Total Recall Training: A Sandancer's Playbook

Tim Jackson

Ring Leader for the UK's Greatest Daycare and Training Centre

Copyright © 2024 by Tim Jackson

All rights reserved. No part of this publication may be reproduced, distributed, or transmitted in any form or by any means, including photocopying, recording, or other electronic or mechanical methods, without the prior written permission of the author, except in the case of brief quotations embodied in critical reviews and certain other noncommercial uses permitted by copyright law.

Published by WriterMotive
www.writermotive.com

Contents

Contents 3

Praise for Our Training and Behaviour Programmes 5

Introduction 10

Chapter One Instinctual Behaviour 17

Chapter Two Nothing in Life is Free..24

Chapter Three Motivation..34

Chapter Four Connection 40

Chapter Five Relationship 44

Chapter Six Engagement 51

Chapter Seven Games..56

Chapter Eight Battle Plan..64

Chapter Nine Circuit Training..66

Chapter Ten Whistle Training...69

Chapter Eleven Letting off the Lead 71

Chapter Twelve The Unleashing Freedom..73

Chapter Thirteen The Sandancer Superhero Dog Club 78

Bonus Section 82

About The Author 84

Other Books by the Author 86

Acknowledgments 87

Praise for Our Training and Behaviour Programmes

What Some of Our Clients Have to Say About Our Training and Behaviour Programmes

"Our three-year-old west highland terrier wasn't responding well to our new shih tzu puppy. We'd expected jealousy etc., but he was really fearful and became aggressive, withdrawn and generally seemed depressed. He'd stopped playing with us, and we were getting to the point of returning our puppy.
Tim came out and spent some time with us and our westie of course, it was us that got the training, lol! Tim was brilliant, gave an honest assessment of our situation and changes we could make immediately, as well as training exercises we could do with the dogs. After perseverance and practice, we now have two happy dogs and the confidence to continue with the work. I can definitely recommend Tim. Thanks so much for a happier life."
Vicki Kenyon

"I joined the Sand Dancer Club when it started a couple of months ago, and I am so pleased that I did. I have known Tim for a while now through puppy class, and some 1-1 training, and my dog loves daycare. The work that Tim has done with Murphy and the advice given has been fantastic. The most telling point for me, as well as seeing the improvements in Murphy's behaviour, is the fact that my dog, who doesn't easily trust people or want them to touch him, loves Tim and will always run over with excitement to greet him!

The Sand Dancer Club has lots of advice as well as lots of fun activities to do with your dog that build on focus and having a great relationship with your dog. For me, one of the best things is that the group is so supportive of each other, offering praise and suggestions when people ask for advice. Tim is always quick to respond to any questions asked. I really enjoy the question-and-answer live sessions as, quite often, the questions others have also result in activities that will help in lots of different situations.

I have enjoyed some really good online training through the Club, which was both fun and informative. Murphy and I love the monthly challenges and learning new things. We are really enjoying the benefits of being in the Sand Dancer Club"
Nicola Mackins

Total Recall Training

"I have a one-year-old Red Cocker and was having a lot of problems with his behaviour – my fault as I totally spoilt him from day one. Tim was recommended by my dog groomer. I rang and booked a telephone consultation. I felt at ease as soon as I spoke to him. He was so lovely and made me feel positive from the start.
We got out of the programme everything we needed. It's up to us now to keep putting in the work we learnt.
After the first lesson, we saw a huge improvement in our dog's behaviour.
I would definitely recommend Tim and Pets2impress."
Sara White

"We bought two puppies and found it extremely difficult to do anything with them; we needed help.
We got in touch with Tim at Pets2impress, who came and did an assessment. He informed us that they had fear-based aggression towards other dogs, and he put our minds at ease, knowing that there was something we could do to help them.
Without Tim's help, I could not have coped. I can't recommend Pets2impress enough ."
Mr and Mrs Selby

"My partner and I adopted a dog from Europe. All was well until three months later when he started to show signs of aggression towards other dogs and men.
We contacted Tim for an assessment and booked him for training. We did everything Tim suggested, and now our dog can be around other dogs (even daycare) and people.
We now have learnt the tools and techniques needed to recognise when our dog is in a situation he is not comfortable with, and we are able to use the training commands to get him out of it, which means no more aggression! Thank you, Tim."
Mr S Scott

"I have a male dog called Storm, who is a Newfoundland cross bullmastiff and has an anxiety issue. He got to the point where he was very fearful of strangers and would growl and bark to scare them off. After several weeks of training with Tim and him bringing various people along to the house, Storm has now started to relax and is nowhere near as bad as he was. I will continue to use Pets2impress with Storm as I can't believe the results they are having with Storm. I am over the moon, and I can now actually start to relax. If you're thinking of using these guys, then it's money well spent."
Lee Brown

"I have absolutely loved taking part in the online course. I love my time spent with Paddy, teaching him new tricks etc., and this course has opened up a whole new load of ideas that I can use and implement in our day-to-day activities that didn't even cross my mind. I thought it was going to be a real struggle for him during this isolation period with the lack of exercise and stimulation that he is used to on a daily basis. He is used to a good 2/3 walks per day as well as 2 – 3 full days at Pets2impress daycare, so naturally, I thought he would be bored during lockdown and bouncing off the walls with energy. During this

course, his tail has never stopped wagging, and I've found that he is just as tired at night during this time as he was after a busy day on the go. Thank you, Tim, for everything you have done."
Samantha Heley

"Having the resources from Tim at Pets2impress available through the lockdown has been invaluable. The changes and help provided have kept our puppy active, stimulated and happy! In a massive change to normal routine, my worry was that Cobie would suffer and lose the confidence that she had gained, but instead, she has learnt so much, and we have the knowledge to keep things going after this is over."

Amy McFaulds

"My Black Labrador Charlie had an amazing time completing the online challenges in the Pets2impress 14-day challenge. He learnt a lot, and so did I. It was both fun and educational! I ordered him the isolation pack so he could get some toys and treats as a reward for his hard work. The pack gave me some more ideas on how to challenge him and train him too."

Anni Jowett

"I would just like to say that Tim came to Stockton on tees yesterday to see my Mam with her dog, Mavis. Tim has made my Mam feel that she can help Mavis, and my Mam isn't upset anymore now that she knows what she needs to do to help her. I'm so thankful for your help. I highly recommend this company; thank you so so much."
Victoria Ainsley

"Thank you so much for all the advice and tips; we definitely have a better-behaved pooch, but still some training to be continued.
To think, just over a month ago, Dave and I were tearing our hair out with a pup who ruled the roost, and life was not enjoyable for any of us including Lara.
You have changed our lives, and since being introduced to you at a web seminar by Katie (dogwood), the combination of training with yourself and scentventure with dogwood, we have a relaxed puppy who is so happy, and we are all enjoying being a family!
I honestly can't thank you enough, and I have already spread the word about Pets2impress to a couple of friends who are thinking of getting a dog.
We will continue our training and advice and keep you updated! Thank you again from all of us, we are finally a family!"
Charlotte and Dave

"Thanks for all your help during lockdown. Training Maverick is a work in progress; we are learning a lot along with Maverick. All your ideas and techniques have been very useful, and we will continue to use them. Life during lockdown with Maverick has been a lot easier. We've had fun, and I think you have saved us a lot of stress. We are happy to recommend you." **Tracie and Stephen Cook**

"Excellent service. Trainer very knowledgeable and explained everything very clearly and showed us how to do training. Very fun sessions with very happy puppies and owners. Very highly recommended" **Cheryl Murray**

"We have been using Pets2impress since its inception. Tim taught our boys to walk on a lead, recall and how to behave as family pets. They've stayed with Tim when we have gone on holiday and loved it. They are walked during the day by Shannon, and I cannot recommend their services enough. Very flexible if you have to make a last-minute change and always happy to help if they can. You've tried the rest… now try the best"
Lesley Elliot – Burn

"I've been a member of the Sandancer Superhero Dog Club with my 16-month-old Border Terrier Bronte since it started, and I can't recommend it highly enough. As with many dogs, Bronte has her own little quirks that make training without proper instruction sometimes quite difficult and stressful. Through the various webinars, games and trick challenges along with Q&A sessions, I am finally starting to really learn about what makes Bronte tick and really respond to me. I have seen such a huge improvement in Bronte's engagement with me when out on a walk, although we still have a way to go, particularly when there are other distractions about. I know that we will overcome the challenges because we have such great support and advice available to us. Tim provides such friendly and useful advice through his various channels, makes himself available whenever you need some additional personal advice, and the support from all the other club members really helps to inspire you to keep on working hard at the training. For me, the Club is a special family, and if you want both you and your dog to be the best that you know you are both capable of, the Club is definitely the Club to join"
Kate Henderson

"I'd like to say that the course has been fantastic. Easy to watch, entertaining and informative. I love the whole idea of engaging our dogs with games when actually out walking! I've always just walked my dogs (I do talk to them all the time tough!), I have allowed them off-leash and had pretty decent recall. Enter Beethoven, and it's a whole new experience! I'm rubbish at the games in the house, mainly because my wee monster follows me everywhere. If I'm busy moving around, he's moving around with me. He only really rests when I do or if I go out!
My go-to with Beethoven off-leash has always been the tennis balls; they are his highest-value treat on a walk. I play the two ball throwing in different directions (can't remember the name!) now, and that really engages him! When I see other dogs or people, I call him back immediately (I find timing crucial!), and I've started playing various games, even funder, which I'd never thought of using on a walk! It works. He's only interested in me!

Tossing the treats in the leaves or long grass, brilliant, he loves it! I have him spinning and sitting and bumping and just anything I can remember! Oh, and the fallen trees, he loves walking along them and jumping over! We've both been having so much fun, and sometimes, he's so tired or contented walking home that we can get past on leash dogs without drama….my nemesis!

I don't know if my waffling here is what you're looking for, but I would say that I found the course most inspiring, practical and simple to follow….I think the key is not to get complacent and stop working; keep the walks fresh and exciting! We can only get better and better. I do feel that when he fails, I've generally failed him first. I see that when I analyse a flop!!! We're not having so many, and I'm certainly much more confident when I go out now. I have a plan and tools to use."

Elaine Coates

"We've really enjoyed Ready Steady Recall. The one-hour webinar each week has been ideal; it fits into the evening after work and has been ideal in that it allows us to practice the activities at our own pace. Your presentation style and humour have really made the course fun and easy to understand. The Facebook group has been very supportive, and it has been so easy to upload videos for feedback. We appreciate your fast response and valuable comments.

We feel we now have the tools and knowledge of how to use them; Archie is so focused on us while indoors; however, as soon as we cross the threshold to the outside world, he has a sensory overload, and we lose engagement. Over the past four weeks, we've definitely seen a massive improvement in Archie's engagement by playing the games outside the house. We need to take baby steps with him, but the improvement we've seen and the experience of completing this course has given us a way forward. We now feel much more positive that we will achieve our goal of enjoyable walks and great recall in the future."

Gill Vardy

Introduction

In agriculture history, goats known as Judas goats once led sheep to their doom.

Sheep are naturally pretty dumb creatures, which makes it difficult to train and herd from one place to another, but strangely, if you add a goat to the mix, they will follow the goat anywhere.

So now there was a way to herd the sheep, but what controlled the goat? How could the rancher guarantee the goat would lead the sheep to the correct area? It turns out that for every herd of sheep deceitfully led to their death, the goat was rewarded with a single cigarette.

Goats are like greedy Labradors and will literally eat anything, so it was not difficult for the ranchers to train the goats once they realised goats like us can become addicted to nicotine.

You may be thinking, what a strange opening story for a book aimed at canine recall; well, what do you think got the goat to where the ranchers needed it to be? Why did the goat keep repeating this behaviour? The answer is simple: the ranchers found something that highly motivated the goat, and dog recall is no different. You too need to find something that motivates your dog if you ever want them to come back to you and stop running off to any distraction they can find.

Taking your dog for a walk should be a fun and enjoyable experience, yet so many owners struggle to keep their dog's attention, and the reason for that is because, in the outside world, life is full of distractions, especially if you are a dog and an opportunist as all dogs are.

From people to dogs, birds, fox poop, squirrels, muddy puddles, cats, smells, and much more, the outside world is full of things that can, will and do easily distract our four-legged friends.

My first dog, Lady, had a pretty good recall despite me not actually doing much with her (I was very inexperienced, shall we say). I struggled with her in many other ways, and if you have read any of my other books, you will know she wasn't the easiest of dogs in her earlier years; however, it is thanks to her unwanted behaviours that I found my passion for training and behaviour, and it is thanks to Lady that I qualified as a Canine Behaviourist.

Despite the traumatic early years, she grew up to be a pretty amazing dog, if I do say so myself. She was with me for 13 years, and the day I had to let her go, I vouched never to get another dog because the pain of losing her was unbearable. As a Veterinary Nurse, I had heard that saying so many times from owners who had their dog put to sleep and then two weeks later, that same owner returned with a new puppy. The reason being is simple: once you let a dog into your life, it is pretty hard to live a life without one, and there is no better love in the world than that you get from your dog.

Two months later, a friend of mine who fostered dogs for a local charity asked if I would look after this little whippet puppy she was fostering. He had been handed into the charity as when he was ten weeks old, he broke his leg, and sadly, the previous owner could not afford the veterinary bills to repair the leg, so he was handed over to the vets and then placed in a foster home. I reluctantly agreed to have him for the weekend; however, if someone hands you a puppy to look after, you are going to fall in love with them and not want to give them back, and my friend knew that….so there you have it, my first whippet. If you asked me four years ago if I would ever get a whippet, it would have been a definite no, not that I have anything against whippets; they were just never the dog I saw myself having.

Lady was a German Shepherd, so having a whippet was the complete opposite end of the scale, but he fit in well into my lifestyle, and I couldn't imagine life without him now. Whippets are sighthounds which were originally bred to hunt primarily by sight and speed. They were bred to pursue prey, keeping it in sight and then overpowering it with their great speed and agility. A whippet's main sense is their sight, and when in chase, they can reach speeds of 40mph.

Now, being a whippet, I knew one thing was for sure, and that was I needed to work on his recall. I knew I didn't want a dog that was able to run up to any dog he wanted, and I knew unless I put in the work at the first glance of a squirrel, he would be off.

How many times has a dog run up to your dog with an owner running, panting away in the background, saying, "It's ok, my dog's friendly"? Whilst Buddy may be friendly, I certainly didn't want to be 'that owner', and I certainly couldn't reach speeds of 40mph on foot, so I needed to make sure that when I wanted him back, he was going to be back by my side.

It took time, and it took patience, and I implemented many of the lessons I am going to share with you in this book; with the help of liver, hotdogs and an old croc, Buddy responded very well to his recall training.

In 2021, I decided one whippet was not enough and decided to get a second whippet, and so we welcomed Bea into our lives who also got a lot of recall training from an early age. Interestingly, what motivated Buddy to get him back to me didn't necessarily motivate Bea and so I had to try different strategies with her, which is normal practice as every dog is different, just like every human is different. What motivates me may not necessarily motivate you.

I enjoy going out on my walks, and I have always been an outdoor person. When I am out with the dogs, I enjoy having them off the lead; however, I don't want my dogs being off lead to cause me stress or embarrassment around other owners. I am forever working with them and forever teaching them that despite all of the amazing distractions out there, I'm their number one, and if they stick with me, then good things will happen. I want them to remember that I am their main value in life, and as dogs spend time where there is value, it was important for me to make sure I am the biggest form of value they can get.

It is the same with the dogs that attend out daycare centre, we take them out on adventures and school trips (true story), picnics, scent adventures and Forest School, but whilst we have them out, we need to be forever working with them and remember that what motivates one dog, may not motivate another so we need to always have plenty of tricks up our sleeve and I'm going to share those tricks with you.

Sadly, so many dogs don't get ample amounts of exercise, and as a result, they put on weight, get bored, frustrated and find un-desired ways to burn off that built-up energy.

Many owners fear letting their dogs off the lead and as a result, keep them on lead but then equally struggle with the dog's constant pulling. I'm not going to be diving into lead training in this book, you can pick up a copy of my other book, Take the Lead for the Perfect Recall for further information on lead training or you can become a member of my inner circle, The Sandancer Superhero Dog Club and gain access to my full online course (be sure to check out the bonus section at the end of this book). In this book, I am going to be sharing everything you need to know for a perfect recall.

Is it going to be easy? Probably not, but is it going to be worth it? Absolutely

The owners I enjoy working with are those who enjoy putting in the work because the more work you put in, the better the result. I am a born and bred Sandancer; it's what us South Shields folk get called. Many people in South Shields are proud of the moniker "Sandancer", and there are numerous different theories, one dating back to the 1850s that describes the skills of the local folk dancing on the sand whilst also helping free ships that had aground on the beach and another theory derived from the terms 'Sans Danger', a reference to the South Shield's history of smuggling contraband of French origin. Regardless of where the phrase came from us Shields folk are proud to be called Sandancers, and I, as well as other dog owners in the area, are extremely lucky in the fact we have many nice places to choose from to walk our dog. If you are from South Shields, local to or in fact planning on visiting for a holiday, be sure to check out the bonus section of the book and download your free dog-friendly guide of South Shields.

Total Recall Training

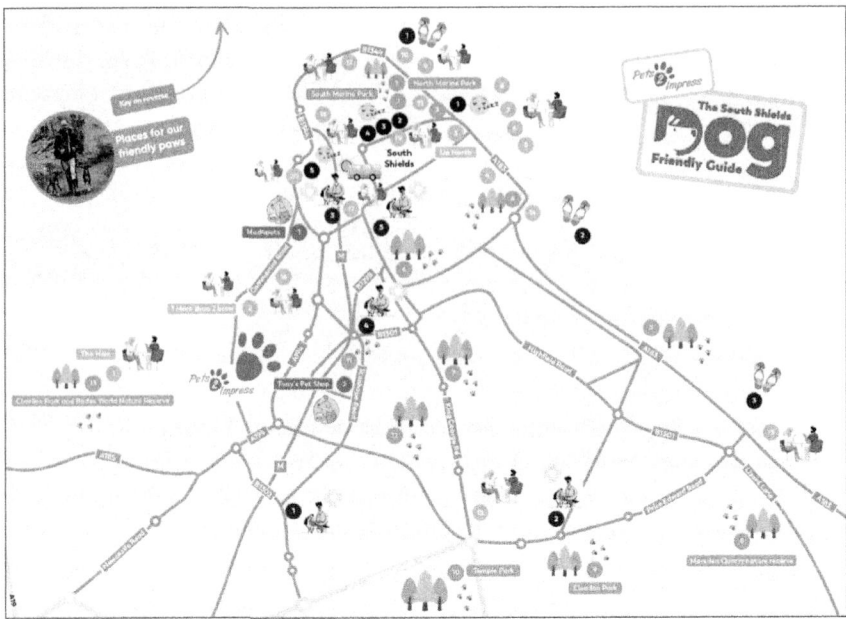

Having the perfect recall takes time, and there are a number of things we need to be looking at to get that perfect recall including motivation, connection, relationship and engagement. Without them, you may as well be pissing in the wind as your dog will find fun elsewhere.

I want to show you the benefits of games and how they can help your dog's recall. I want to show you how to have a better relationship with your dog, and I want to show you that a walk isn't just walking to the field, standing in one spot and throwing a ball for your dog.

Being outside should be all about you and your dog, not worrying about replying to emails or catching up with your friends on the phone. These things can wait and should wait because when you are out with your dog, they should be your number one priority.

We need to remember that dogs spend a huge proportion of their day indoors with very little enrichment, so when they do get the opportunity to be outdoors, it is very fun and exciting and easy for them to lose focus, but it doesn't need to be like that and I am going to help you achieve that perfect recall, but it is important to point out now that I promote positive based methods of training, I do not believe in punishment including shock collars, spray collars or in fact any other negative based methods of training, so if that is what you are looking for, I suggest you look elsewhere. I learnt the hard way that negative methods of training never correct the problem, and I want to help you correct the problem as I know the benefits being off lead can have for our dogs and I want your dog to live a happy life.

In 1880, Newcastle marked the endpoint for numerous ships entering the Tyne. Recently, my exploration led me to the discovery of the High and Low lights situated in North Shields and South Shields. Despite residing in South Shields my entire life, I had never taken notice of these landmarks. While in North Shields with my children, visiting The Stan Laurel Statue in Laurel Park (both my son and I are avid Laurel and Hardy fans), we glanced over the Tyne toward South Shields and spotted two similar structures – the high light and the low light. Intrigued, I delved into the history of these lights, completing construction in 1808 and first illuminating the lanterns on May 1, 1810. Towering one above the other, they serve as the Tyne's prominent navigation points, guiding ships safely into Shield's Harbour, steering clear of hazards like the Rock End, the Black Middens, Prior's Stone, and the Herd Sand – perilous obstacles marking the submerged remains of numerous ships and sailors. These present lights replaced an earlier pair constructed in 1727.

Think of me as The High and Low lights, guiding you down a secure and successful path to achieve the perfect recall. Many pet owners often make the error of turning to online search engines for solutions to their dog-related challenges. However, the abundance of conflicting information they encounter can lead to confusion, exacerbating the issues they face. Similar to the High and Low Lights guiding ships into the harbour, there was also Jingling Geordie, who, in the 1720s, lit a fire in the mouth of a cave beneath Knotts Flats. His intent was to confound ship captains and cause shipwrecks, allowing him to plunder the cargoes and personal items washed ashore. His legend persisted into the 1930s.

Just as mariners were cautioned against falling for Jingling Geordie's deceptive tactics, dog owners are advised not to bewilder themselves by exploring myriad recall solutions online. Instead, embrace the guidance provided in this book to relish pleasant walks with your canine companion once more.

There is no point in reading this book and then putting it on the shelf and thinking, 'Oh, I enjoyed that' (Don't worry, you will enjoy it). You need to put in the work and understand that any form of training can take time and will always require a lot of patience.

I would advise you to focus on one chapter at a time. Read that chapter and then start working through the lessons in that chapter before progressing to the next chapter.

Are you ready to learn? Are you ready to have a perfect recall?

Great, you are in the right place; let's get started, shall we?

Chapter One
Instinctual Behaviour

Dogs can be our very best friends, and let's face it, they make the world a better place. They are our family members and our closest companions. But before the 1800s, dogs were primarily selected for functional roles such as hunting, guarding and herding. Although now we think of our dogs as cuddly little buddies, they still have many instinctual behaviours. Instinctual behaviours in dogs are inherent and automatic responses ingrained in their genetic makeup, shaped by centuries of evolution. These behaviours are hardwired survival mechanisms that enable dogs to navigate and thrive in their environment.

With proper training, dogs are capable of learning a whole host of commands, from sitting and speaking to more complex skills. The dogs within my online club, The Sandancer Superhero Dog Club, amaze me every day with their skills and learning capabilities. Personally though, I find it is the behaviours we don't teach that can be the most fascinating and probably the most frustrating for many owners.

Dogs are like all animals and are born with a range of instinctual behaviours which develop because they serve the dog in some way. Some common instinctual behaviours seen could be digging holes, which, let us be honest, is not great for our gardens, but for dogs, it could be a way for them to express themselves, or it could be an easy way for them to gain some much-needed mental and physical stimulation. Dogs can dig for fun because they are stressed, bored or to relieve anxiety. Dogs may also be following their natural urge to create a den for shelter and comfort, whilst others are more predisposed to digging because some breeds, such as terriers, were bred specifically to dig prey out.

Another common instinctual behaviour seen is the guarding of people or various items. Let's be honest; we all have that one dog in the street that you can't pass the house without all hell breaking loose. Just like other animals, dogs develop a natural instinct to protect things that they class as valuable, for example, food. The way they express this instinctual behaviour can vary from dog to dog but often can include growling, barking, lunging or stiffening. The main purpose of the behaviour is simply a desire to keep the thing that they class as valuable.

Then we have sniffing of the butts; this is certainly something we do not train our dogs to do but something 99% of dogs do. It's instinctual and a traditional greeting for dogs; thankfully, we don't greet each other that way. Can you imagine the first time you meet the in-laws and you sniff their butt to say hello? Yikes.

Saying that, my first impression of my in-laws was not much better; no, I didn't sniff their butts, but I was warned that I would be offered a glass of whiskey, and although I didn't like whiskey, I still had to accept it and drink it. So, my first time visiting the in-laws, I get offered that said glass and I necked it back with a look of horror on the father-in-law's face. The Mrs comes in and says, "where is your whiskey?" to which I replied, "Oh, I drank it, it was lovely". I have never been able to live that moment down; they say first impressions are important....ooops. You kind of had to be there really, and although I know nothing about whiskey, I do believe it was an expensive bottle and certainly not one that should be necked back in one go.

Anyways back to butt-sniffing as this is another instinctual behaviour and an important one when you are a dog because dogs can learn a lot of useful information from another dog's butt. Secretions from a dog's anal glands contain certain information about the animal's identity, gender, mood, diet and overall health – impressive, right?

There are so many instinctual behaviours that we don't teach, yet dogs do on a daily basis, turning around before lying down, burying bones and other items, and rolling in disgusting things such as fox poop or, in my dog's case, dead birds.

Instinctual behaviours can be frustrating, and they are there whether we like them or not. To get a better understanding, let's have a look at some breeds to see what they were originally bred for.

The pointer was originally bred to find prey animals. Their job was to locate and, I guess, kind of point to say, "Here it is, I've found it". I was once working with a lovely pointer, doing some recall work down at Marsden Beach, and her recall was pretty spot on; however, she kept finding dead birds and made sure to let us know they were there, much to the owner's disgust.

Then we have cocker spaniels, a very common pet of today. These were originally bred to hunt small prey, in particular birds called woodcocks, which is also a part of their name. They would run into the bushes and scare the birds into taking flight, and then it was fair game for the hunters to shoot them (the bird, not the dog). Ever wondered why cocker spaniels love chasing birds or heading off into the bushes? It's instinctual, and they do it because they enjoy it; in fact, they get rewarded internally for doing so.

Bloodhounds were bred for tracking for their incredible sense of smell. They would originally track deer and wild boar. When I worked for Dogs Trust, I once had to microchip 30 Bloodhounds, which were used for human tracking. It was pretty impressive watching these dogs in action, and I absolutely love Bloodhounds, so that was an added bonus and a great day at work for me.

Border collies were originally bred to herd, Dachshunds were bred to hunt badgers, Mastiffs were used for guarding, greyhounds were bred for their eyesight and footspeed to help catch fast prey, St. Bernards were bred for search and rescue, Yorkshire terriers for vermin control, Poodles were used to catch waterfowl and Golden Retrievers, used to retrieve waterfowl that had been shot.

The list literally goes on, and these are just a few examples; however, I am sure your dog will display certain behaviours that you have not taught them to do; these behaviours will be instinctual behaviours.

Drawing an analogy between dogs and computers can offer a clearer perspective on their composition. In this comparison, dogs are akin to computers, each equipped with their unique hardware, analogous to different breeds such as pugs, Jack Russels, or German Shepherds. Similarly, computers possess software like Word or Excel, while in dogs, the software represents everything they learn from birth. Additionally, both entities share a component known as firmware. In computers, firmware is an intrinsic part that cannot be erased, and in dogs, it is mirrored by their DNA, a fundamental genetic code that remains unalterable. This DNA forms the basis of their instinct, an inherent drive that compels them to engage in characteristic canine behaviours. Understanding these parallels provides insight into the complex yet fascinating nature of dogs, emphasizing the combination of genetic predispositions and learned behaviours that shape their personalities.

Instinctual behaviour is actually just a simple stimulus-response behavioural mechanism. For example, consider the way a bird cares for her chicks. The sight and sound of a chick begging for food triggers the instinctive feeding response in the mother bird. The mother bird does not think about what she is doing; she naturally has the inclination to respond to her chick's cues. For a mother bird's first brood, do you think she is able to read a book to find out how to be the perfect mother? I hope you answered no, as unlike us, birds do not have health visitors or midwives; they lay their eggs, instinct is to keep them warm until they hatch, and then instinct helps them feed the birds up before they are ready to fly the nest.

Snakes have instinctual behaviours to hunt despite never meeting their parents. They survive because they have instincts that are pre-installed into their DNA before they are born.

Sea turtles hatch on the beach, yet after hatching they have an instinctual behaviour to walk to the ocean. This hasn't been taught, its pre-programmed into them.

The Story of Sable the Zebra

In the vast Serengeti plains of Africa, a herd of zebras roamed freely, each member attuned to the primal instincts of survival. Among them was Zara, a young zebra with distinctive black and white stripes. One day, as the herd grazed peacefully, a distant rumble echoed across the plains.

Without hesitation, the zebras lifted their heads, ears perked, and nostrils flaring to catch the scent carried by the wind. The leader of the herd, an experienced mare named Sable, sensed an approaching danger. Her instincts, honed by years of living on the savannah, told her that predators were nearby.

Sable let out a warning whinny, a unique call that signalled an imminent threat. Instantly, the zebras formed a tight-knit group, with the young ones in the centre and the stronger adults forming a protective barrier on the outskirts. Their coordinated movements showcased the instinctual understanding of safety in numbers.

As a group of lions emerged from the tall grass, the zebras, guided by their instinctual behaviours, executed a synchronized response. They kicked up dust, creating a barrier between them and the predators, while Sable led the charge, herding the herd away from the danger.

The lions, realising that their chances of a successful hunt were slim, abandoned their pursuit. The zebras, now guided by their instincts to remain vigilant, continued their journey across the Serengeti, a living testament to the power of innate behaviours honed through generations.

This story illustrates how instincts drive collective behaviours within animal communities, ensuring their survival in the unpredictable and often harsh conditions of the natural world.

The Story of Luna and Her Pups

In the heart of a dense forest lived a family of wolves led by the wise and experienced Luna. One day, as the pack ventured through the woods in search of prey, Luna's keen senses detected a subtle shift in the air. Instinctively, she knew that danger lurked nearby.

Her fur bristled, and she emitted a low growl, signalling the pack to halt. Luna's intuition guided her to a hidden threat - a silent, camouflaged snake coiled in the grass, poised to strike. The pack, trusting Luna's instinctual wisdom, maintained a safe distance, their hackles raised in response to the unseen peril.

However, Luna's youngest pup, Zara, driven by curiosity, inched forward toward the snake. The pack, watching with bated breath, observed Luna's rapid response. In a split second, Luna dashed forward, her jaws snapping shut just inches away from Zara. The snake slithered away, and Zara, startled but unharmed, learned a crucial lesson about the dangers lurking in the forest.

This incident showcased the instinctual behaviours ingrained in the wolf pack. Luna's ability to sense danger, the pack's immediate response to her signals, and the protective nature displayed towards the vulnerable pup all highlighted the primal instincts that governed their lives in the wilderness.

As the pack resumed its journey through the forest, Luna's leadership and the instinctual unity of the wolves remained a testament to the deep-seated behaviours that ensured their survival in the wild.

These are just examples so you can see how some behaviours are primarily just there; we don't train them into our dogs; they are born with them, which is why instincts are powerful things. They subconsciously shape many of our dog's behaviours which is why it is so important that we have a

Total Recall Training

better understanding of our dog's instinctual behaviours to help give them some kind of outlet.

So the next time you have to bath your dog after he has rolled in something smelly, just remember that's his instinct. When he shakes all that mucky water all over you, despite you telling him 100 times not to remember that too is instinctual behaviour that they can rarely hold back.

So why do we need to know about instinctual behaviours when it comes to recall? Sadly, it's the failure to provide some kind of outlet for our dog's drive (or instinct) that causes so many issues. If we don't give our dogs the opportunities to display these instinctual behaviours, then they will go off and find ways to do it themselves, which is why we have so many owners screaming and shouting for their dogs when off the lead. Want to know more about instinctual behaviours? You need to become a member of my online community and my inner circle, The Sandancer Superhero Dog Club. Inside, you will gain access to my ready, steady recall course and a special teleclass I delivered regarding predatory motor patterns. You can sign up via my website, www.pets2impress.com

Good news, you don't need to move to a farm because you own a herding dog, and you don't need to apply for your gun license because you own a gun dog. There are many other ways to keep your dog occupied and focused on you, and if you follow my golden rules, you will soon be the envy of your town.

There are five golden ingredients for a perfect recall, and those are

- Motivation
- Connection
- Relationship
- Engagement
- Games

Lately, my son has developed a newfound enthusiasm for baking after indulging in episodes of Junior Bake Off. This newfound interest has sparked his love for creating delicious treats in the kitchen. Just like the essential ingredients required for a perfect Victoria Sponge cake—caster sugar, butter, eggs, self-raising flour, baking powder, milk, icing sugar, jam, and vanilla extract—each component plays a vital role. Similarly, when aiming for the ideal recall with our furry companions, it's crucial to consider various ingredients, metaphorically speaking. These include a strong connection, effective training methods, engagement activities, and a deep understanding of our dog's needs. Each element contributes to the overall success, much like the blend of ingredients that ensures a delightful Victoria Sponge cake. In essence, just as the absence of a key ingredient affects the outcome of a baking endeavour, overlooking any aspect of recall can hinder achieving a perfect connection with our dogs.

Before we can get into the nitty-gritty tips for success, we need to go right back to the foundations and start as we mean to go on by introducing a learn-to-earn programme, and that is just what we will be discussing in the next chapter. Everything starts from the foundations; when we first started school (seems a long time ago for me), one of the first things you learn is how to read and write, and we need that in order to progress further and learn more and to help us in the world we live in and just like us dogs too need their foundations. Now I'm not going to be teaching your dog how to read and write in this book (maybe the next one), but I am going to advise you to strip everything back and go back to the basics.

Chapter Two
Nothing in Life is Free

Dogs love to earn, and they are naturally very attention-seeking little creatures; however, if dogs do not learn the value or earning things, then how can we expect them to walk nicely on a loose lead, remain calm when visitors come round, toileting outdoors or in this case how can we expect them to have that perfect recall?

We need to start as we mean to go on, so to begin with, we need to introduce a programme called 'Nothing in life is free', or in other words a learn-to-earn programme.

One of the nicest things you can do for your dog is to increase their confidence and independence, and by implementing a 'Nothing in life is free' programme, you will do just that. Plus, you will teach your dog that if he wants something, he has to work for it.

Dogs love to learn, and they love to work, and by encouraging your dog to do that, you automatically increase confidence and independence and set your dog up for success.

Now nothing in life is free doesn't mean we have to send them to work every day or get them to wash the car, pick up the shopping or crack on with the housework. It basically means if the dog wants something, he has to do something in order to get it.

Think of it this way: why do we go to work? Personally, I love work, but for most, it is to get paid at the end of the month. You have to put in the work to get what you want in the end. Or think of a vending machine, the first thing you have to do is put in your money, and then once you have done that, you get the reward i.e. the sweets or the can of Pepsi.

Imagine an employee consistently meets project deadlines and exceeds performance expectations. In response, the manager publicly praises the employee during a team meeting, highlighting their dedication, hard work, and the positive impact they've had on the team. Additionally, the manager may award the employee with a certificate of achievement or a bonus as a tangible acknowledgement of their exceptional efforts. This positive reinforcement aims to motivate the employee to continue demonstrating high levels of performance and meeting deadlines in the future.

As of now, your dog should work for everything, so for example, if he wants his dinner, have him sit or wait first; if he wants to go for a walk, get him to sit; or if he wants to play with the new exciting toy you have just bought for him get him to lie down.

Personally, I do not mind what you get him to do, but he should do something in order for him to get something. Think of it like teaching a child to say please and thank you.

Everyone in the household needs to follow the same rules, as this programme will not only make your dog more confident and more independent but also help with all aspects of your dog's training.

We also need to put a stop to any attention-seeking behaviours, and let me shout this loud and clear… I am not saying you cannot love your dog, and I am certainly not saying you should not give your dog attention… what would be the point in having a dog?

We just need to make sure that all attention is invited by us and not the dog so, for example, imagine being sat on the settee on a night time watching television (I can't lie, it would be Coronation Street or Eastenders for me!) and the dog comes and plonks one of his toys on you, waiting for you to throw it. This would be classed as attention on his terms; therefore, we should ignore these behaviours. You may find that the dog tries his hardest to get your attention and may try new behaviours to see if those gain your attention, but it is very important that this is ignored.

There are three very important lessons to remember when it comes to ignoring your dog: 1. Do not look, 2. Do not touch, and 3. Do not speak – by breaking any of those rules, you may as well put him on his back and give him a belly rub just for being cute.

If say, after 30 minutes, he gives up and starts to walk away, and providing you want to, which I am sure you will, call him to you and give him lots of fuss and attention and, by all means, spend the rest of the evening playing with him, cuddling him, kissing him… whatever you like to do really.

So, by doing it this way, we can still give the dog attention, but now it is on our terms and not on the dogs.

It is not a case of trying to punish the dog as many would see it; in fact, it is the opposite. We are implementing these steps to help build up confidence and independence, and we are teaching the dog that it's ok not to have attention from Mam or Dad every second of every day, I can quite happily entertain myself.

As humans, we tend to fixate on the negatives, and this inclination is often mirrored in how dog owners approach working with their canine companions. Rather than dwelling on undesirable behaviours, it is more effective to shift our focus towards positive reinforcement. Consider a scenario where a dog barks at a passerby through the window – a common situation where owners may react negatively. Instead, I encourage you to embrace a positive reinforcement approach. Allocate a daily "value pot" by setting aside 50 pieces of your dog's daily kibble allowance. Strategically place these pots around your home. The objective is to actively observe and reward your dog for positive behaviours throughout the day. Recognise moments of calmness, resting in their bed, or refraining from barking. By emphasizing positive actions and redirecting attention away from negative behaviours, you create an environment where your dog associates good behaviour with rewards. Over time, this reinforces desired behaviours, leading to a more well-behaved and contented canine companion. Remember, the key lies in promoting positive actions rather than inadvertently reinforcing negative ones. By following this approach, you are likely to witness a positive transformation in your dog's behaviour, making Tim Jackson's book an invaluable resource for fostering a harmonious relationship with your furry friend (and don't forget to share your positive experiences through a stellar 5-star Amazon review).

That is the first important change you must make moving forward. Now let us have a look at another very important aspect: a routine.

Dogs are creatures of habit, and they love to predict what is coming next; we know the importance of a routine. We only need to think of how much our routines were thrown out the window during the COVID-19 Pandemic.

Dogs, like us, respond very well to routine and structure. Naturally, we want to keep things fun and exciting for the dogs too, so I always advise a varied routine, and I will explain what I mean by that now.

A routine for dogs should consist of five things (these do not need to be set in stone, i.e. you must walk your dog at a certain time, you must do training at a certain time; it is more a case of thinking each day I need to ensure my dog gets the following activities throughout the day) and these are:

1. Feeding Times

Ideally, our dogs should be fed twice per day, and normally, this would be at a similar time each day. Now I don't advise varying the diet, but I would advise varying the way you feed your dog.

Make feeding times fun, and make your dog work for his meals. I very rarely use a food bowl for my dogs, Buddy and Bea, instead I get them to work for their food, so this could involve placing their food in a Kong toy, a scatter feed in the garden, a homemade brain game or a puzzle game you can buy from the shops.

In fact, sometimes, I even use their daily allowance and do a training session with them.

We cannot forget food is a reward; therefore, they need to work for it (Nothing in life is free) so ask your dog to 'sit' and 'wait' first before releasing them. By spicing up mealtimes, you encourage your dog to work for their food, and in the process, your dog is getting mentally stimulated, which is a great way to help burn excess energy off your dog, which will ultimately help with your dog's recall training and in fact any other training you are doing with your dog.

One of Buddy's favourite games is to hang his Kong from the washing line. It takes him a long time to get the last bit of kibble, and he is always shattered afterwards… win-win. This is a great activity if I am trying to get the children ready for school because it keeps him occupied whilst I get the children ready for school.

As with any form of mental stimulation, every 10 minutes equivalates to a 45-minute on lead walk, so by the end of the day, I have two very sleepy and calm dogs. In the bonus section of this book, I have included a free handout called recycle the recycling, which will give you some great starting points to help spice up mealtimes. You can add to these and make them more difficult too.

Now we can have a look at the second part of your dog's daily routine.

2. Walk Times

It goes without saying dogs need to be walked every day, not just when the weather is fine! Walks are fun for your dog, and they give your dog the chance to make use of their natural senses, i.e. touch, smell, taste, sound and sight.

Walks give your dog a change of scenery. Imagine being stuck indoors day in and day out with no form of interaction... no doubt you would get bored pretty quickly, which naturally would have an impact on your well-being. The same applies to dogs, and it is mostly dogs that lack a lot of exercise that develop behaviour or training issues. Once again, if we look back at the dreaded lockdowns, we have to endeavour during COVID-19. Being stuck in the house was not fun, especially when I had one dog and three children to entertain at the time.

Dogs do not have the luxury of popping out when they like. They rely on us as owners to take them out. Walks shouldn't just involve heading to the field to throw a ball; you should be making every walk into an adventure – certainly something we do at Pets2impress with the daycare dogs; in fact, our daycare dogs go out on adventures, picnics, forest school, school trips and scent adventures.

Later in this book, I will be discussing how you can make a 1-hour walk feel like a 4-hour walk for your dog.

3. Training Times

In an ideal world, we should be spending 3-4 times per day for 5-10 minutes training our dogs. This is a massive confidence builder and will massively help to reduce anxiety in your dog. Always start the session with something you know your dog can do reliably well and always end the session with something your dog knows, as this helps to keep the sessions positive.

In-between, start to teach your dog new things. Trust me, when it comes to training your dog, you can be as imaginative as you like as long as you and your dog are both having fun; nothing else matters.

Regular training sessions are a great way to reinforce the Nothing in life is free programme, and in fact, it will help encourage your dog to want to work more for things which, that's right, you guessed it, will help with your dog's recall training and any other aspect of training you are working on.

During training times, you should also implement some form of brain game such as a puzzle game or scent work as the two work hand in hand together, and both will play a huge part in reducing your dog's energy levels as well as helping to build confidence. I have included a free webinar in the bonus section of this webinar, which was presented to the members of my online training club, The Sandancer Superhero Dog Club. The webinar will give you an introduction to scent work and how you can implement it into your dog's day-to-day routine. Engaging in scent work with dogs provides a myriad of benefits, tapping into their innate olfactory abilities and stimulating their mental and physical well-being. This activity not only channels their natural instincts but also offers a constructive outlet for their boundless energy. Scent work enhances a dog's problem-solving skills as they learn to locate specific scents, promoting mental stimulation and preventing boredom. It fosters a stronger bond between the dog and its owner, as collaborative scent-based activities create opportunities for teamwork and shared accomplishment. Additionally, scent work serves as an excellent confidence booster for dogs, reinforcing their sense of accomplishment when successfully completing scent-related tasks. Moreover, it is an adaptable and accessible activity that can be tailored to dogs of all ages and abilities, making it an inclusive and enjoyable experience for our canine companions.

I often like to advise something I call 'recycle the recycling', which basically means if you are about to throw something in the recycle bin, STOP and think, "can I make this into a brain game for my dog?" The answer is normally yes, and it's so simple to do but has unlimited benefits for your dog.

An example would be a toilet roll tube; cut it up into rings and then interlock those rings together to make a ball shape, post a couple of treats within and then bingo, you have a homemade brain game.

Seconds to create but lots of fun for your dog. If he destroys it, who cares, it was going in the recycling anyway. Do not forget in the bonus section of this book, there is also a free download available, which will give you a number of starting ideas of how to make some great and simple brain games for your dog.

During the first lockdown, I introduced a 14-day online challenge for owners to take part in with their dogs. Each day, they were given a new challenge, which involved either teaching a new trick or creating a brain game. The feedback from this challenge was crazy, one client said:

Total Recall Training

"I have absolutely loved taking part in this group challenge. I love my time spent with Paddy, teaching him new tricks etc., and this group has opened up a whole new load of ideas that I can use and implement in our day-to-day activities that didn't even cross my mind. I thought it was going to be a real struggle for him during this isolation period with the lack of exercise and stimulation that he is used to on a daily basis. He is used to getting 2-3 good walks per day as well as 2-3 full days at daycare per week, so naturally, I thought he would be bored and bouncing off the walls with energy. Being part of this group has been great for him; teaching him new tricks and doing things such as jumping over toilet rolls has really helped tire him out both physically and mentally. His tail has never stopped wagging, and I've found he is just as tired at night during this time as he was after a busy on the go day."

Now bearing in mind at the beginning of the lockdown, we were restricted to one bit of exercise per day. Because the above owner implemented the training, she learned from the online challenges she still had a tired and happy dog by the end of the day… with less exercise than normal.

During the initial lockdown, I found myself with a single canine companion, Buddy, accustomed to a bustling routine that included morning walks, accompanying me to work, exploring our unique scent space tailored for dogs, engaging in various adventures, participating in training sessions, and concluding the day with a brief stroll before dinner and bedtime. Recognising that the mandated one-hour daily exercise allowance wouldn't suffice for Buddy's energetic nature, I redirected my focus indoors, dedicating more time to training activities. The 14-day challenge seamlessly transitioned into an online course named 'The Isolation Station,' eventually evolving into 'Dancing with Dogs.' While I never envisioned teaching my whippet to dance, the joy he experienced during these sessions far exceeded any expectations. Although his dance routines may not have met Britain's Got Talent standards, witnessing Buddy revel in the fun is a testament to the positive impact these unconventional activities had on our lockdown experience. You can catch glimpses of Buddy's dance routines through the following links:

https://youtu.be/W48rCe5JSx4?si=kkT7G0R4GQ84bMBo
https://youtu.be/3P-OXCWOBq8?si=Sph21Ufg6ZZe-6Hr
https://youtu.be/RKRO16xpW6c?si=Nebc7TbKZfoXXS4t
https://youtu.be/Nmjx6oK-Ty4?si=_xsLkMOpBAuVmssE

As I have said, they are by no means Britain's Got Talent standards, but he had a lot of fun, and I certainly had a lot of fun teaching him some new tricks.

To really help reduce your dog's anxiety, to build up confidence and independence, I cannot stress how important regular training sessions are with your dog. Do not forget these too should be varied, so do not just focus on the same training sessions each day; trust me, your dog will get bored. This now moves us on to the next part of the routine. Why not sign up to become a member of The Sandancer Superhero Dog Club and check out my online dancing with dogs course? Maybe your dog will make it onto Britain's Got Talent.

4. Regular Playtime

As with the training sessions, you want to aim for a minimum of 3-4 playtime sessions per day with your dog, each session being around 5-10 minutes long.

Vary the toys that you play with, and don't forget rule number 1: if the dog wants to engage in some playtime with you, then he needs to work for it and why? Because nothing in life is free!

Buddy, as like most dogs, has numerous toys but I only ever leave out 3-4 at any one time. I rotate these toys every couple of days to give him something new to play with and to keep things fun and fresh for him.

During our playtime sessions, I bring out one of his special toys. I then asked him to sit, and once he had, we continued with our play session.

This is a part of the day that Buddy adores, his favourite toy being an old crock, which now does not really resemble any form of footwear, but he loves it, and I make use of this on numerous occasions, believe it or not, it's my go-to item to get him back to me when he is off lead because when he sees that nothing else matters.

Any form of active play helps keep your dog's heart healthy, keeps the joints lubricated, and improves their overall balance and coordination. Active play sessions also have a huge impact on a dog's mental health, keeping them happy, building confidence and, most importantly, keeping anxiety levels down.

When choosing toys for your dog, always try and aim for ones that encourage your dog to make use of their natural senses, for example, toys with various textures or toys that can be stuffed with treats, such as the Kong range.

Remember, playtime should be fun for you and your dog, and it's a great way once again to build on that strong bond you already have with your dog. If you find a toy your dog adores and a toy that really motivates your dog, then this toy should be coming out with you on walks. You don't just have to rely on treats all the time; variety is always the way forward.

We are now ready to move onto the final part of the routine, a very important aspect of any dog's routine.

5. Quiet time

If you implement the above (which you should), naturally it will tire your dog out a lot more than he is used to; therefore, it is very important that he is able to rest throughout the day. Dogs should have their own space that they can go to for some chill time. This could be a bed or a crate, but somewhere where the dog feels safe and secure.

We know what our moods are like. If we don't get a good night's sleep, we can be moody, argumentative, angry, emotional… the list goes on. Dogs too, like us, need their sleep.

Imagine what effect it would have on you if your sleep was disturbed every night. I'm a father of 4; trust me, I know!

If your sleep pattern keeps getting disturbed, then this will have a huge impact on your mental well-being and energy levels. A dog that doesn't get enough downtime can become very stressed and anxious, and it can play a massive part in their day-to-day life and, in some cases, can lead to aggression as the dog gets frustrated a lot quicker or less tolerant.

Make sure when your dog goes to his bed, he is not disturbed. If you have children at home, then make sure his sleeping area is away from the children and actively encourage your dog to have a little nap. All four of my children know that if Buddy or Bea are in their bed, then they shouldn't be disturbed… I wish Buddy and Bea would follow the same rules when I am in bed.

Dogs love to know what is coming next, and throughout this chapter, we have discussed the foundations of what you need to implement to ensure your dog gains confidence and independence and burns off energy indoors. Next, I want to look at a very important lesson, and that lesson is what motivates your dog. To have a reliable recall, you need to equip yourself with things that motivate your dog.

Chapter Three
Motivation

As I prepared for the European Karate Championships in Italy, I couldn't help but reflect on the importance of motivation in achieving success. Just like humans, our furry friends, our beloved dogs, are driven by unique motivators. Understanding what truly inspires them is the key to unlocking their full potential, especially when it comes to training a reliable recall.

Motivation is a powerful force that propels us forward, pushing us to reach new heights. For me, I love karate, Netflix binges, a meal out, and spending time with my children, family and friends. These are some of my main motivators. They ignite a fire within me, fuelling my determination to excel in my chosen endeavours. When I first started karate following the release of Cobra Kai, a very popular Netflix series following on 30 years after the original Karate Kid movie, it was not just about aiming for the black belt but more so working my hardest to be the best I could be, especially given the fact I am older and not as flexible as I once was. However, I was and still am motivated to do the very best I can.

Similarly, dogs are motivated by a myriad of factors that can vary from one individual to another. What excites and drives one dog may not have the same effect on another, just like you may not be motivated by karate as I am. That's why discovering their unique motivators is essential when training a reliable recall.

Just as I religiously attend karate training sessions two to three times a week, I understand the importance of consistency and practice in honing my skills. Dogs thrive on routine and repetition too. Regular training sessions provide them with structure and help reinforce positive behaviours.

However, it's crucial to remember that not all dogs find the same activities motivating. While one might leap at the opportunity to chase a ball, another might be more inclined to work for tasty treats or playtime with their favourite toy. Every dog has their own set of preferences, and it's our responsibility as pet parents to uncover what truly drives them and excites them.

In July 2023, I participated in the European Karate Championships in Italy, an event that I dedicated months of training to. Just as I've tailored my training regimen to suit my goals and motivations, it's important to personalize the training approach for each dog.

Some dogs find treats to be irresistible rewards, while others may respond better to verbal praise or a game of fetch. By experimenting with different motivators, we can uncover the key that unlocks our dog's potential and ignites their enthusiasm for recall training.

The European Karate Championships was a defining moment for me, showcasing the culmination of my hard work, dedication, and motivation. Similarly, discovering and utilising what motivates your dog will lead to a successful recall training journey. It will strengthen the bond between you and your furry friend while also ensuring their safety and well-being.

So, as you embark on the adventure of recall training, remember that each dog is a unique individual with their own set of motivations. Be patient, observant, and open-minded as you explore what inspires your four-legged companion. Celebrate their progress, embrace their quirks, and together, unleash the incredible potential that lies within them.

In our busy household, raising four children has been a delightful adventure (sometimes a challenging one too), each one uniquely motivated by their distinct passions and interests. Sienna, our soon-to-be 13-year-old, finds inspiration in the captivating world of TikTok (much like her Dad) and the enchanting realm of makeup (not so much like her Dad). Her creativity shines through as she experiments with various makeup styles, showcasing her skills and artistic flair and often leaving a huge mess in the bathroom after applying her fake tan. If someone can explain the fascination of fake tan to me and why so many people feel they need as I do not get it…however, this proves my point: what motivates one person may not motivate another.

Harvey, on the other hand, is a bundle of energy and enthusiasm. His world revolves around the discipline of karate, the intricate world of Lego construction, and the fascinating realms of Science and Maths. It's incredible to witness his dedication and focus in these areas, a testament to his inquisitive mind and physical prowess. He amazes me with his quick thinking when it comes to his times tables (actually, it's more putting me to shame as it takes me a lot longer to think of the answer than it does him).

Total Recall Training

Darcey, the artistic soul of the family, is captivated by the simple joys of playing with her dolls and expressing herself through drawing. Recently, she discovered a newfound passion for karate (this made me very happy), adding an extra layer of excitement to her vibrant personality. Although she occasionally enjoys letting out a spirited scream, it's all part of the lively symphony that defines Darcey; however, I do not think the neighbours quite agree, especially at 5am in the morning.

Last but certainly not least, we have Alfie, affectionately known as our own little "Wreckit Ralph." His world revolves around the magnetic allure of trains, the zooming fascination of cars, and, of course, the joyous chaos that ensues when creating delightful messes. Alfie's infectious energy and curiosity keep us all on our toes.

Our household is a vibrant tapestry of diverse interests and passions, with each child contributing their unique thread to the family narrative. While they share commonalities in their love for sweets and Dad's Yorkshire puddings, their individuality is celebrated and encouraged. After all, it's these differences that add colour and richness to our family dynamics, making every day a new and exciting chapter in our shared journey and adventure together.

Just as my children have unique motivations, dogs too possess individual preferences and desires. Understanding what motivates your dog is like unlocking a treasure trove of possibilities, enabling you to tailor their training and strengthen the bond between you.

To find what truly inspires your furry companion, embark on a journey of observation and experimentation. Watch closely as they interact with their environment, toys, and treats. Notice the activities that make their tail wag with joy, and their eyes gleam with excitement. Does your dog go wild for a game of fetch, or do they revel in a tasty treat? Are they more motivated by praise and affection or by the opportunity to explore and discover new scents?

Much like South Shields, where a harmonious blend of cultures and experiences enriches our community, dogs come from diverse backgrounds and carry their own unique histories. Adopted or rescued dogs may have different motivators and triggers compared to those raised from puppyhood. Take their past experiences into account as you uncover their motivators, allowing you to create a safe and supportive training environment.

One approach to discovering your dog's motivators is through the power of positive reinforcement. By offering rewards that align with their individual preferences, you can encourage and reinforce desired behaviours. Just as the seafront in South Shields draws people from all walks of life, find the reward that speaks to your dog's heart, whether it's a tasty treat, a favourite toy, or a loving pat on the head.

Remember, finding what motivates your dog is an ongoing process, much like the evolving tapestry of our vibrant town. As you embark on this adventure, celebrate every small victory and observe the subtle cues that reveal their preferences. Embrace their unique personalities and let their motivations guide your training journey.

Whenever I discuss motivation with clients, whether that be on a 1-1 basis or to the members of The Sandancer Superhero Dog Club (see the bonus section of this book for your FREE trial), one particular story always comes to mind. Around two years ago, I was running an outdoor puppy school lesson where owners took their previous learning skills on lead and recall out to the real world. I had four puppies off lead on a busy beach with lots of other people around. Three of the puppies were doing amazing, but one was paying no attention to her owner. This particular puppy had done amazing inside the class in our training arena, but outside, there was just too much temptation for her. The owner had her whistle, the dog's favourite treats and the dog's favourite toys, and she tried all sorts to get this dog back to her.

It was clearly frustrating, and the owner wanted to get the puppy back on the lead and call it a day. My response was 'NO'; we need to find something other than what you have that is going to motivate the puppy, and so I picked up a feather. I wiggled the feather around and started acting the clown, jumping up and down and guess what happened? The puppy lost interest in everything else and had all eyes on me…or the feather! I found something that motivated the puppy and then handed the feather to the owner and to her surprise her puppy stayed by her side, engaging with her and I believe from that day forward, the magic feather that we called it went everywhere with them, success!

So where can you start finding what motivates your dog?

Dogs, much like us, are driven by various motivations, and understanding what truly captivates your furry friend is the key to successful training. One of the most common motivators is food, a universal language that transcends species. To unearth your dog's culinary preferences, set up a simple yet revealing exercise. Take an empty muffin tray and fill each cup with different treats—bits of chicken, hotdog slices, dog treats, kibble, or even carrot chunks. Observe your dog's behaviour. Does it dive into an open buffet, delicately choose a favourite, or inhale the entire spread in one enthusiastic snort? Take notes, for each action unveils valuable insights.

Identifying your dog's favourite treat is crucial. Create another tray, incorporating the favoured treat from the first round alongside eleven new ingredients. Does your dog remain loyal to the initial choice, or does a new contender emerge? Repeat until a clear winner surfaces, a treat that will become your secret weapon in recall training.

For some dogs, toys are the magic wands of motivation, especially outdoors; for others, they are more motivated by toys, so now we need to think of a way to find your dog's number 1 toy. Dump your toy collection on the floor and observe. Does your dog gravitate towards a particular toy? Repeat the exercise to confirm its preference. This chosen toy becomes your ally in outdoor recall training, a safer alternative to chasing after dogs or squirrels.

Reflect on your dog's unique motivators beyond treats and toys. Does it revel in being fussed over? Respond positively to verbal praise? Exhibit joy through the simple act of sniffing? These details are the building blocks of effective recall training.

As already mentioned, my dog Buddy revealed an unexpected fondness for a specific croc shoe. When taken outside, the croc became the focal point of undivided attention. There have been many times when I have stupidly forgotten the croc, and so I grab a shoe off one of the kids. It works, and the kids find it hilarious, so it's a win-win. This illustrates the importance of experimenting with different motivators to find the one that resonates with your dog.

In conclusion, the key to successful recall training lies in understanding and leveraging your dog's motivations. What you assume motivates them may not align with reality. Be open to surprises, experiment, and find that golden motivator that will transform your recall training into a seamless and rewarding experience for both you and your furry companion.

So now we have found what motivates our dog? What is the next ingredient needed for a perfect recall? The next chapter will dive into connection and the importance of having a great connection with your dog. If you don't have a connection with your dog, how can you expect them to want to come back to you, especially when there are so many other exciting distractions out there?

Chapter Four
Connection

In the first quarter of 2023, the UK witnessed 27,465 final divorce orders, shedding light on the unfortunate reality of relationships reaching their breaking point. While various factors contribute to the dissolution of marriages, a notable aspect is the breakdown of connection between couples. The significance of a strong emotional connection cannot be overstated in maintaining a healthy and enduring relationship. Couples often find themselves drifting apart when communication falters, emotional intimacy diminishes, and the sense of connection weakens. A lack of shared experiences, understanding, and emotional support can erode the foundation of a relationship, making it susceptible to the strains of life. The ability to communicate openly, empathize with one another, and actively nurture the bond is vital in fostering a resilient connection. As the divorce statistics highlight, prioritizing and continuously working on the emotional connection within a relationship is crucial for its longevity and the overall well-being of both partners involved.

Just like connection is an important element of marriage, it is also a key part of having a great recall. If you don't have a connection with your dog, how can you expect them to want to come back to you, especially when there are so many other exciting distractions out there? With connection, you get

- Trust
- Confidence
- A dog that wants to come back to you

Connection can easily be achieved by spending more time with your dog and interacting with them. Connection shouldn't just be something you do outdoors. You need to be connected before you even step outside. By connecting with your dog before you even start your walk, you are helping to burn off some built-up energy. How many times have you shown your dog his lead, and how many times has he gone wild at the pure thought of going out for a walk? By allowing your dog to get this excited, you are immediately starting your dog's walk off on a negative. It may be worth reading another book I wrote, 'Take the Lead for the Perfect Recall' as this will give you some useful insights into how to start your walk off on a calm.

In a nutshell, we want to be spending 10-15 minutes before we leave the house engaging in some form of activity with our dog, whether that be some scent work (see bonus section of the book for your free webinar, An introduction to scent work), basic training, trick training, puzzle games etc.

This is a simple way to burn off some excess energy, as a 10-minute brain game is equivalent to a 45-minute walk; it tires a dog out more to use their brain than it does to use their physical energy; naturally, the two work together. By playing a game with your dog before you leave or engaging in a fun activity, you are teaching your dog that you are fun to be around and guess what? This will encourage them to continue to want to be around you. Later in this book, I will be sharing some simple fun games that you can play to help keep that focus on you when the time comes to removing that lead.

In the intricate dance between a dog and its owner, one fundamental element stands out as the key to unlocking obedience and trust: the connection between them. Recall the ability to bring your dog back to you on command is not just a training command; it's a reflection of the bond you share. In this chapter, we'll delve into the profound importance of fostering a strong connection with your canine companion and how it directly correlates with a reliable recall.

Understanding the Canine-Human Bond:

Dogs are inherently social animals, driven by an instinct to form close bonds with their pack members. When we invite them into our lives, we become an integral part of their pack. However, this bond isn't instantaneous; it requires time, effort, and mutual understanding.

Your dog's connection with you goes beyond mere training routines; it's a deeply emotional and psychological link. Establishing this connection builds a foundation of trust and loyalty that significantly influences your dog's responsiveness to your commands, particularly recall.

Trust as the Cornerstone:

Trust is the cornerstone of any healthy relationship, and the human-canine bond is no exception. When your dog trusts you, they are more likely to view your recall command not as an imposition but as an invitation to safety and security. Trust is built through positive interactions, consistent training, and a genuine investment in understanding your dog's needs and preferences.

Building trust involves being a reliable and consistent presence in your dog's life. From daily routines to unexpected situations, your dog should associate you with a sense of security. When trust is established, your dog will be more inclined to respond promptly to your recall command, knowing that returning to you is a positive and rewarding experience.

Communication Beyond Words:

While dogs don't speak our language, they are remarkably attuned to non-verbal communication. Your body language, tone of voice, and overall demeanour convey a wealth of information to your dog. When working on recall, it's crucial to pay attention to the signals you're sending; this is a reason a whistle works really well in recall training, which is something we will touch upon later in this book.

Maintain a calm and inviting posture when calling your dog, and use a friendly and encouraging tone. Dogs can pick up on your emotions, so approaching recall with patience and positivity enhances the connection. The more attuned you are to your dog's body language and cues, the better you can adapt your communication to strengthen the bond between you.

Shared Experiences:

Creating shared experiences goes a long way in forging a connection. Whether it's daily walks, playtime, or exploring new environments together, these shared moments contribute to a sense of companionship and shared purpose. Dogs thrive on routine, but they also benefit from novel experiences that stimulate their minds and strengthen their bond with their owners. This is one of the reasons our award-winning daycare is so popular as the novel experiences the dogs get whilst in our care have them thirsty for more.

Incorporate recall training into these shared experiences. Instead of viewing it as a separate, isolated command, integrate recall into play sessions or outings. This not only reinforces the training in a real-world context but also associates the recall command with enjoyable activities, making your dog more eager to respond.

Positive Reinforcement and Rewards:

Positive reinforcement is a powerful tool in building a strong connection with your dog. When it comes to recall, rewarding your dog for returning promptly reinforces the behaviour and cultivates a positive association with obeying the command. Remember we discussed our daily pot of value and rewarding the desired behaviours and ignoring the unwanted behaviours?

Use high-value treats, praise, and affection as rewards for a successful recall. This not only reinforces the behaviour but also reinforces the positive emotions tied to the act of returning to you. Over time, your dog will associate recall with positive outcomes, strengthening the connection between you.

Addressing Challenges:

Building a strong connection and achieving a reliable recall is not without its challenges. Dogs, like humans, are individuals with unique personalities and quirks. Understanding and addressing challenges, such as fear, distraction, or past negative experiences, is crucial in overcoming obstacles in your journey to a reliable recall.

Patience and Consistency:

Patience and consistency are virtues in dog training, especially when it comes to recall. Building a strong connection is a gradual process that requires time and dedication. Consistent training sessions, positive reinforcement, and a patient approach will yield long-term results.

In the tapestry of canine training, recall is a thread intricately woven with the connection between a dog and its owner. The strength of this bond determines not only the reliability of recall but also the overall harmony in the human-canine relationship. As you invest time and effort in building a strong connection with your dog, you're not just teaching a command; you're nurturing a bond that transcends words and commands, creating a partnership built on trust, understanding, and mutual respect.

As well as having a good connection with your dog you also need to have a good relationship with your dog, and that is what we shall be talking about in the next chapter. Thinking of that yummy Victoria Sponge cake and the ingredients needed to create said cake, connection is another necessary ingredient, as is having a good relationship.

Chapter Five
Relationship

Imagine we are sitting in a DeLorean, driving 88 miles per hour and travelling back in time to the year 1930, when the dreaded dominance theory was first introduced. The word dominance is a word I very rarely use, and when I hear someone say it, my skin crawls, and I know I've some human educating to do before I can make a start on training the dog. The sad truth is so many people believe their dogs are trying to dominate them, trying to take over the house, trying to be dominant around other dogs. Answer me this! Why on earth would your dog want to be more powerful or successful than you? Correct me if I am wrong, but do you feed your dog? Do you walk your dog? Do you buy your dog new toys and treats? If your dog does any of the above, then please give me a call, I would love to hear about it!

Why would a dog want to dominate you when you provide everything for them? When you start to think of it like that, it now seems a bit silly, doesn't it? (I can hear you saying, "Yes, Tim"). The issue with the dominance theory is so many owners believe that their dog is trying to achieve higher social 'status'; therefore, to correct this, the owner needs to establish 'dominance' over the dog and implement it as part of their training plan.... BIG FAT, NO NO!

I can all but guarantee that implementing the dominance theory will end up resulting in one thing: you get bitten, and the dog gets put to sleep! I hate to be so black and white, but I see and hear this day in, and day out. So where did the dominance theory come from? There was a study carried out on wolves in captivity. Now it is important to remember that these wolves were not related, and they were all placed into one enclosure and observed for behaviour. The evidence gathered showed that these wolves fought over resources such as food, sleeping areas and mates, and the studies suggested that there was a hierarchy system in place with the 'alpha' (the leader) having first dibs at everything.

Therefore, they were branded as a dominant species, and because dogs were believed to have descended from wolves, then they too were branded as a dominant species that were trying to take over our households and be the 'Alpha' of the pack… what a load of dog poo!

Very recently, thanks to modern technologies, we are now able to get up close to wolves in the wild (I love a bit of David Attenborough!), and there is no evidence to suggest that wolves are a dominant species; they live very similar to the way we do as a family, and they work together as a family to ensure the survival of the pack. Instinctual behaviours play a pivotal role in the survival strategies of wolves, particularly concerning the protection and nurturing of their offspring. In the wild, wolves exhibit innate behaviours geared towards ensuring the well-being and survival of their young. This includes the establishment of dens for shelter and protection, as well as the formation of tightly-knit family units within a pack. The pack structure enables cooperative hunting and communal care for the vulnerable pups. Female wolves, in particular, demonstrate maternal instincts, dedicating themselves to nursing, grooming, and safeguarding their progeny.

You may have worked with 'trainers' in the past that have mentioned how you need to establish the alpha role within your household if you want to have a better-behaved dog. Let us have a look at some examples of the methods of training that these 'trainers' advise people to implement, and you let me know your thoughts!

- Pin your dog down to the floor if he is 'misbehaving' and hold him there until he is calm
- Eat before your dog
- Leave a room before your dog
- Be more assertive with your dog
- Take your dog's food away as they are eating, so he knows 'you are the boss.'

You must agree this is not what we envisioned when we got a dog, right? The problem with the dominance theory (apart from it being a huge pile of dog poop) is it causes stress for your dog and, in a lot of cases, can cause fear. Please correct me if I am wrong, but this is not why we got a dog; we got a dog to be a part of the family and to be loved. I do appreciate that at times when you are at the end of your tether, you want results, and you want results now, but I hate to break it to you; that's not how it works with dog training. Dog training requires time, patience and consistency. If you implement this form of training is it any wonder your dog doesn't want to come back to you when off the lead? Would you?

In the United Kingdom, the professions of dog training and behaviour consulting are currently unregulated, posing a challenge for pet owners seeking reliable guidance for their canine companions. Unlike some regulated professions, anyone can proclaim themselves a dog trainer or behaviourist, emphasizing the importance of cautious selection when seeking professional assistance. Aspiring dog trainers may or may not possess formal qualifications or certifications, making it crucial for pet owners to inquire about the trainer's educational background, experience, and any relevant certifications they may hold. The absence of regulation means that a variety of training philosophies and methods coexist within the industry, and some trainers may still adhere to outdated dominance-based approaches. When seeking a trainer or behaviourist, it is advisable for pet owners to prioritize individuals who stay abreast of contemporary, evidence-based training methods and avoid those who rely on antiquated dominance theories that have been debunked by modern behavioural science. A vigilant approach to choosing a professional ensures that pet owners find trainers who use humane, effective, and scientifically supported techniques to foster positive behavioural changes in their canine companions. I could have saved myself a lot of time and effort training and working hard to become a canine behaviourist; however, when I first set upon this journey, my aim was to help people and, most importantly, help dogs (it still is don't worry) and for me to do that I wanted to ensure I practised up to date evidence-based training and have the necessary qualifications under my belt.

Beyond the realm of training commands and obedience lies a richer and more profound aspect of the human-canine relationship — a connection built on mutual respect, empathy, friendship, compassion, sacrifice, compromise, non-verbal communication, patience, dedication, and unconditional love. In this chapter, we'll explore the importance of cultivating these qualities in your relationship with your dog and delve into practical ways to strengthen this extraordinary bond.

Mutual Respect:

At the core of a healthy relationship with your dog is mutual respect. This involves recognising your dog as an individual with feelings, needs, and preferences. Respect is a two-way street; just as you expect your dog to follow your commands, it's essential to acknowledge their autonomy. This acknowledgement fosters a sense of trust and equality, laying the foundation for a harmonious partnership.

Empathy:

Empathy is the ability to understand and share the feelings of another. In the context of your dog, it means being attuned to their emotional state. Dogs are highly sensitive to human emotions, and by empathizing with your furry friend, you create a safe space for them to express themselves. Recognising when your dog is anxious, excited, or content allows you to respond appropriately, strengthening the emotional connection between you.

Friendship:

A true friendship with your dog goes beyond the roles of owner and pet. It involves companionship, shared experiences, and genuine joy in each other's company. Cultivating a friendship with your dog means being present in their life, participating in activities together, and celebrating the unique bond you share.

Compassion:

Compassion involves a deep understanding of your dog's needs and the commitment to meet them. Whether it's providing comfort during times of distress or attending to their physical well-being, practising compassion builds trust and reinforces your role as a caregiver.

Making Sacrifices:

A strong relationship often requires sacrifices. This could mean adjusting your schedule to accommodate your dog's needs, foregoing certain activities to spend quality time together, or making decisions that prioritize their well-being. These sacrifices underscore your commitment to the relationship and deepen the sense of trust.

Compromising:

Just as in any relationship, compromise is key. Understanding your dog's preferences and finding common ground in activities and routines contribute to a balanced partnership. Flexibility and compromise create an environment where both you and your dog feel valued and understood.

Non-Verbal Communication:

Dogs are masters of non-verbal communication, relying on body language, facial expressions, and vocalizations to express themselves. Understanding and responding to these cues is crucial for building a strong connection. Pay attention to tail wags, ear positions, and posture as they reveal valuable insights into your dog's emotions. In 2023, I ran a two-part teleclass discussing canine body language, and you can check it out when you sign up to become a member of my online club, The Sandancer Superhero Dog Club. Still not a member? Head to the bonus section of this book NOW.

Patience:

Patience is a virtue, especially in the realm of dog ownership. Training, behaviour modification, and the development of a strong relationship all require time and patience. Embrace the journey, recognising that progress may come in small steps. Patience fosters a positive and stress-free environment for both you and your dog.

Dedication:

Building a lasting relationship with your dog demands dedication. This means consistently investing time and effort into their well-being, training, and overall happiness. Dedication is the glue that holds the fabric of your connection together, reinforcing your commitment to your furry companion.

Unconditional Love:

Perhaps the most profound aspect of the human-canine relationship is the presence of unconditional love. Dogs don't judge, hold grudges, or place conditions on their affection. Embracing this pure form of love strengthens the bond between you and your dog, creating a source of unwavering support and companionship. I will always remember the day I had to let my lovely dog, Lady, go; one of the hardest things I ever had to do. I took her for a walk to her favourite place, Trow Rocks in South Shields. From a young age, she always loved being there, and I spent some time there with her on her last day, reflecting on the time we had spent together and thinking of this strong relationship we had built over the years and despite a rocky start with her behaviour issues and my lack of anything dog-related once we got over that hurdle we had the most perfect relationship, something I still carry with me today almost six years since I said goodbye.

Practical Ways to Strengthen the Relationship:

1. **Spending Time Together:** Devote quality time to activities you both enjoy. Whether it's walks, playtime, or simply lounging together, shared experiences create lasting memories.
2. **Clear Communication:** Establish clear communication through consistent cues and commands. Use positive reinforcement to convey your expectations and celebrate your dog's successes.
3. **Love in Their Food:** Infuse mealtime with love by preparing nutritious and tasty meals. This not only nourishes their body but also becomes a ritual of care and affection, and be sure to spice up the way you feed your dog too.
4. **Training Sessions:** Regular training sessions strengthen the bond and improve obedience. Make it a positive and enjoyable experience for your dog, incorporating rewards and praise.
5. **Playtime:** Play is a vital component of a dog's life. Engage in interactive play to foster a sense of joy and connection. Different dogs have different play preferences, so find activities that resonate with your furry friend.
6. **Calm Presence:** Dogs are incredibly intuitive. Maintain a calm and composed demeanour, especially in challenging situations. Your dog will look to you for guidance and reassurance.
7. **Understanding Likes and Dislikes:** Pay attention to your dog's preferences. Some dogs enjoy cuddling, while others prefer more independent activities. Respecting their likes and dislikes strengthens the understanding between you, plus you can play in their likes when it comes to recall training.
8. **Speak Dog:** Learn to 'speak' your dog's language. Understanding their vocalizations, body language, and signals enables effective communication, reinforcing the connection (don't forget to check out part 1 and part 2 of the speak dog teleclasses inside the vault of The Sandancer Superhero Dog Club).
9. **Touch:** Physical touch is a powerful way to express love. Regular grooming, massages, and gentle pats create a sense of security and strengthen the bond.
10. **Exercise and Mental Stimulation:** Physical exercise and mental stimulation are essential for a well-rounded, happy dog. Tailor activities to your dog's breed, age, and energy level to keep them physically and mentally engaged.

The relationship between a human and their dog is a tapestry woven with threads of mutual respect, empathy, friendship, compassion, sacrifice, compromise, non-verbal communication, patience, dedication, and unconditional love. As you continue with this journey with your dog, remember that building a strong relationship is an ongoing process that requires time, effort, and a genuine commitment to understanding and appreciating the unique qualities of your furry friend. The rewards of a deep and meaningful relationship with your dog extend far beyond obedience and training, creating a bond that enriches both your lives in ways that words cannot fully capture.

Chapter Six
Engagement

If you want a reliable recall from your dog, not only do we need a connection, not only do we need a good relationship, but we also need engagement.

Engagement needs to start with us as the human. If you want your dog to choose you, then you need to prove that engaging with you is the best thing ever; you need to prove you are way more exciting than any other distractions out there. By engaging with your dog, you can help discover and access behaviours that your dog enjoys doing.

Engagement with your dog transcends the traditional notions of obedience and commands. It is a dynamic and reciprocal interaction where both you and your canine companion actively choose to participate, creating a bond that goes beyond routine boring walks and training sessions. In this chapter, we'll explore the significance of engagement and how it forms a two-way street where your dog willingly chooses to connect with you and ignores everything else that is going on around him. We'll delve into making walks more than just a stroll, transforming them into exciting adventures that captivate your dog's interest and enthusiasm, keeping all eyes on you.

The Essence of Engagement:

At the heart of engagement lies the idea that your dog actively wants to be involved with you. It's not just about following commands but about the genuine joy and enthusiasm your dog exhibits when interacting with you. This choice to engage fosters a deeper connection and a sense of partnership where both you and your dog contribute to the dynamic. Right now, it may seem like you will never get your dog to come back to you, but if you are actively engaging with your dog out on walks and leaving your phone in your pocket, there is a much higher chance they will stay with you and keep their focus on you, especially if you are giving them something they want.

Dog Choosing to Engage:

When your dog chooses to engage, it signifies a level of trust and enjoyment in your presence. This choice is a powerful indicator of a healthy and vibrant relationship. It's about creating an environment where your dog feels motivated and excited to interact, recognising you as a source of fun, comfort, and fulfilment and not needing to run up to every other dog in sight or chase every squirrel they see.

Making Yourself the Most Rewarding:

For engagement to flourish, you must become the most rewarding aspect of your dog's world. This involves understanding your dog's preferences and tailoring interactions to align with their interests. Whether it's through play, treats, or affection, being attuned to what motivates your dog ensures that they actively seek out your company.

Participation and Involvement:

Engagement isn't a one-sided affair; it requires active participation from both ends of the lead. Encourage your dog to take an active role in the interaction, whether it's through games, exploration, or shared activities. This mutual involvement strengthens the sense of connection and makes the experience more enriching for both of you.

Making Walks More Than Just a Walk:

Transforming your daily walks into engaging adventures is a key aspect of fostering connection. Instead of a routine stroll, consider the walk as an opportunity for exploration and shared experiences. Incorporate elements that capture your dog's curiosity and stimulate their senses.

Parkour on Walks:

Introducing elements of parkour into your walks adds an exciting dimension to your dog's physical and mental stimulation. Parkour involves navigating and interacting with the environment creatively. Encourage your dog to jump over obstacles, balance on surfaces, or navigate through natural elements. This not only provides physical exercise but also enhances their problem-solving skills. If you follow Pets2impress on Facebook, you will see parkour is something we like to do a lot with our daycare dogs and why? The answer is simple: it keeps their attention on us.

Training on Walks:

Engage your dog's mind during walks by incorporating training exercises. Simple commands, recall practice, or trick training can turn a routine walk into a dynamic learning experience. This mental engagement is as vital as physical exercise for your dog's overall well-being.

Scent Work:

Dogs have an incredible sense of smell, and incorporating scent work into your walks taps into their natural instincts. Hide treats or toys along the route and encourage your dog to use their nose to find them. This not only provides mental stimulation but also deepens the bond as your dog associates the walk with an enjoyable and rewarding activity. This is one thing I love about scent work: it's portable, and you can do it anywhere.

Adding Variety:

Dogs thrive on variety, so break away from the monotony of the same routes. Explore new neighbourhoods, parks, or trails to keep walks fresh and exciting. Novel environments engage your dog's senses and contribute to a more enriching experience.

Daycare Adventures:

Reflecting on our practices at Pets2impress Dog Daycare, we understand the importance of engagement in every outing. When we take our daycare dogs for walks, it's not just about exercise; it's about creating an adventure that captivates their interest. We encourage exploration, provide opportunities for social interaction, and ensure that each dog actively participates in the outing. If we didn't do that, then walks wouldn't be much fun for us either, especially with the added responsibility that we are walking other people's dogs as well.

Promoting Engagement at Daycare:

At daycare, engagement is at the forefront of our interactions with the dogs. We observe their individual preferences, create stimulating environments, and foster a sense of camaraderie among the pack. This approach not only ensures physical exercise but also nurtures a positive and engaging atmosphere that dogs eagerly anticipate.

Encouraging Social Interaction:

Dogs are social animals, and their engagement extends to interactions with other dogs. Daycare outings are structured to allow dogs to engage in play, socialization, and shared activities, reinforcing the sense of community and connection among the pack. One thing you do need to consider, though, is that not every dog likes other dogs, so it is wise not to allow your dog to run up to every dog they come across, hence why having a strong level of engagement works wonders.

Embracing Variety:

Just as with individual walks, variety is essential during daycare outings. We explore different parks, trails, and play areas to offer a diverse and stimulating experience for the dogs. This variety not only keeps the dogs engaged but also prevents boredom and promotes mental well-being.

Inviting You to Explore South Shields:

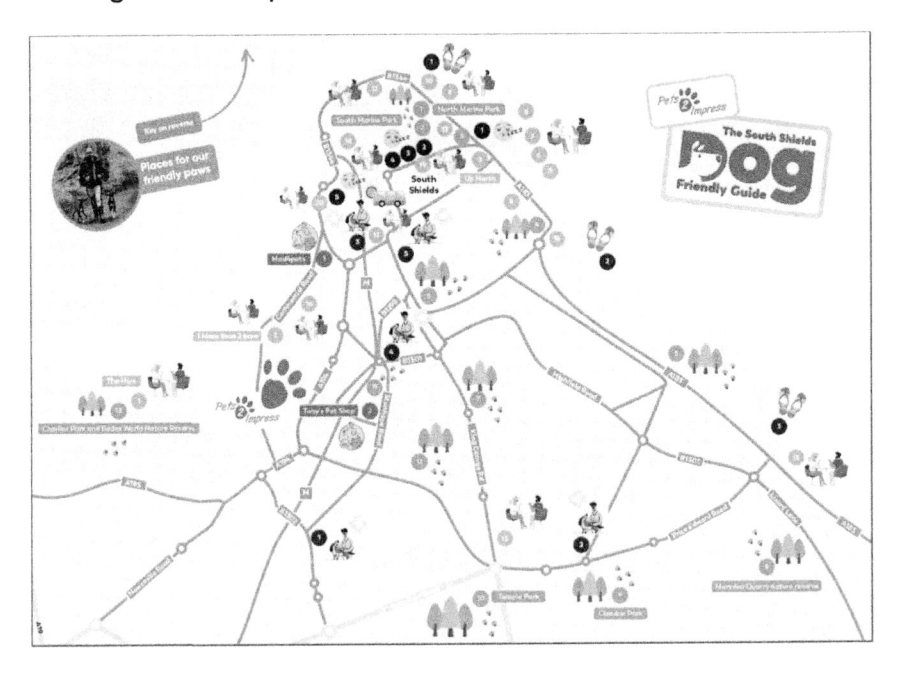

If you're in South Shields, enhance your walks by downloading my free dog-friendly map from www.pets2impress.com. Explore the local parks, scenic routes, and dog-friendly spots to add variety to your outings. Discovering new environments together contributes to a shared adventure that strengthens your connection.

Engagement is the heartbeat of a vibrant relationship with your dog. When both you and your canine companion actively choose to connect, the bond deepens, and the shared experiences become more meaningful. By making walks more than just a stroll, incorporating elements of parkour, training, scent work, and embracing variety, you create an environment where your dog eagerly participates in the adventure of daily life. Whether on individual walks or daycare outings, the essence of engagement lies in the joy, enthusiasm, and mutual involvement that defines the unique connection between you and your furry friend

Chapter Seven
Games

In the era preceding the advent of mobile phones (I am telling my age now, I promise I am not that old), my childhood was filled with the joy of engaging in various outdoor games and board games that helped create a lovely childhood. Classic childhood games such as "What's the Time, Mr Wolf?" and "Polo" were certainly my favourites, offering endless hours of laughter and excitement. I was also a huge fan of kiss chase; however, that game would more than likely be frowned upon today, but at the time, I loved counting to ten and then chasing after all the girls to see which one I could kiss. Not to be forgotten is the perennial favourite, "Knocky Door Neighbours," a game of stealth and surprise that added an extra layer of thrill to our outdoor escapades as well as pissed off many of our neighbours, but I am sure they got over it. Christmas, for me, has always been a time of joy and togetherness, and as a child, it always brought forth a treasure trove of board games that became a cherished tradition in our household. Games like "Hungry Hippos," "Frustration," "Monopoly," and "Jenga" were unwrapped with eager anticipation, promising hours of friendly competition and bonding. While many are familiar with classics like Monopoly™ and Scrabble™, it's fascinating to learn that the roots of board games trace back to ancient Egypt, around 5,500 years ago, and have since evolved across diverse cultures and societies. Beyond the sheer enjoyment they bring, research underscores the pivotal role of games in fostering healthy development, allowing children to not only apply what they know but also encouraging them to experiment, find solutions, develop strategies, and, most importantly, build confidence and skills that extend far beyond the game board. The nostalgia of those childhood games remains a testament to the enduring power of play in shaping memories and fostering growth, and just as games play an important part in any child's life, the same can be said for playing games with your dog.

Not many owners understand the importance of playing games with their dogs. Games can help build confidence, reduce anxiety, they help build on your relationship with your dog, help build trust and offer a great outlet for your dog to display their natural instinctual behaviours in a way we as humans class as acceptable. Games show that you are fun to be around; they help your dog lose focus on any other distractions around them because they are too busy having fun with you. Games help with obedience and impulse control and it is a perfect combination to keep your dog entertained and fit.

I am going to share a number of different games you can play with your dog to help with their recall training. Practice indoors to begin with, and then when your dog is happy and knows the rules of the game, you can start to take them outdoors.

Not all of these games will motivate your dog, so if your dog has no interest in some of the games, then don't use them. You want to be equipped with games that your dog will want to engage with and get involved with; otherwise, it would be like someone trying to get my attention with a game of chess, and I would lose interest very quickly.

Play is a universal language that transcends species, and for dogs, it serves as a powerful tool for learning, communication, and relationship-building. In this chapter, we'll delve into the myriad benefits of incorporating play into recall training. By understanding the transformative impact of games, you can turn routine training sessions into dynamic, enjoyable experiences that strengthen the bond between you and your four-legged friend.

The Inherent Joy of Play:

Dogs are natural-born players. From puppyhood to adulthood, play is not just a recreational activity for them; it's an essential component of their overall well-being. Recognising and embracing the joy that play brings to your dog's life is another step in leveraging its potential for recall training.

Building a Positive Association:

Play creates positive associations with various activities, and recall training is no exception. When you infuse training sessions with elements of play, you're shaping your dog's perception of the recall command. Instead of viewing it as a formal instruction, your dog associates it with an exciting, enjoyable interaction, making them more likely to respond enthusiastically.

Enhancing Motivation:

Games serve as powerful motivators for dogs. Whether it's chasing a ball, engaging in tug-of-war, or participating in a hide-and-seek session, the inherent fun in these activities becomes a reward in itself. By making the recall training session a game, you tap into your dog's intrinsic motivation, making them eager to participate and respond to your commands.

Physical and Mental Stimulation:

Play provides a holistic form of stimulation, addressing both physical and mental needs. Recall training games that involve running, jumping, and problem-solving not only keep your dog physically fit but also engage their cognitive abilities. This combination is essential for a well-rounded and satisfied canine companion.

Strengthening the Bond Between You and Your Dog:

The shared joy of play strengthens the bond between you and your dog. When you actively participate in games, you become a source of fun, excitement, and companionship. This shared experience fosters a sense of connection and partnership, creating a positive environment for effective recall training.

Relieving Stress and Anxiety:

Play is a natural stress reliever for dogs. Engaging in playful activities helps alleviate anxiety, channel excess energy, and promote relaxation. When recall training is approached as a game, it becomes a stress-free, enjoyable experience for your dog, reducing any potential apprehension or resistance.

Adapting to Different Learning Styles:

Dogs, like humans, have diverse learning styles. Some may respond better to visual cues, while others are more attuned to physical activities. Incorporating various games into recall training allows you to adapt to your dog's preferred learning style, making the training process more effective and enjoyable.

Fostering a Positive Training Environment:

Traditional training methods can sometimes be perceived as formal or disciplinary. The introduction of play transforms the training environment into a positive, dynamic space. Your dog associates training with play, creating an atmosphere where they are more likely to actively participate and respond to your cues.

Boosting Confidence:

Success in play, whether it's retrieving a toy or solving a puzzle, boosts your dog's confidence. This confidence extends to recall training, where a positive association with responding to your command enhances your dog's self-assurance and willingness to engage in training activities.

Improving Focus and Attention:

Playful recall training games inherently improve your dog's focus and attention. When a game is introduced, your dog's attention becomes laser-focused on the activity at hand. This heightened focus carries over to the recall command, making it more likely that your dog will respond promptly and attentively.

Adventurous Explorations:

Games often involve elements of exploration and adventure. Whether it's a game of hide-and-seek or an agility course, incorporating these adventurous aspects into recall training turns routine sessions into exciting escapades. This not only enriches your dog's daily experiences but also reinforces the recall command in various contexts.

Transitioning to Formal Commands:

While play provides an informal and enjoyable context for recall training, its benefits extend to the transition to more formal commands. Once your dog has established a positive association with the recall command through games, you can seamlessly integrate these commands into everyday situations, ensuring a reliable response in various environments.

Tips for Incorporating Play Into Recall Training:

1. **Know your Dog's Preferences:** Understand your dog's favourite games and activities. Tailor recall training to incorporate elements that align with their preferences, ensuring a higher level of engagement.
2. **Use High-Value Rewards:** Reinforce positive behaviour during games with high-value rewards. This could be treats, praise, or additional playtime, making the experience more rewarding for your dog.

3. **Keep Sessions Short and Dynamic:** Dogs thrive on variety, so keep recall training sessions short, dynamic, and engaging. Incorporate different games to prevent monotony and maintain your dog's interest.
4. **Gradual Progression:** Gradually increase the difficulty and complexity of games as your dog becomes more proficient in recall. This ensures that the training remains challenging and interesting.
5. **Safety First:** Choose games and environments that prioritize safety. Be mindful of your dog's physical capabilities, and ensure that toys and play areas are safe and suitable for their size and breed.

What Games Can You Play With Your Dog?

Remember every dog is different, and what motivates one dog may not necessarily motivate another dog. It is about finding a good variety of games that keep your dog motivated and focused on you, so despite what is going on around them, you are their number one focus. We will now look at a number of different games to play, and if you want to know more, then I urge you to take advantage of your free bonus in the bonus section of this book to join my online community, The Sandancer Superhero Dog Club where you will gain immediate access to my online lead and recall courses.

The 'Name' Game: Begin your training sessions with the delightful 'Name' game. Indoors, say your dog's name in a cheerful tone and praise them. This simple exercise counters negative associations, creating a positive link to their name. Extend this game outdoors, reinforcing the joyful connection at least five times before allowing them off the lead. Say their name, and then give them a treat; get that focus before you even think about letting them off the lead. Ensure a happy and upbeat atmosphere during the exercise, and stop using their name in a negative way; trust me, it won't help you in the long run.

The 'Shadow' Game: Transform walks into an engaging experience with the 'Shadow' game. While on a lead, encourage your dog to catch up to you, rewarding them when they do. If they get ahead, turn around 180 degrees, patiently waiting for them to join you. Reward, walk away, and repeat. The objective is to have your dog willingly follow you, reinforcing recall in an interactive manner.

Hide-and-Seek: Engage your dog's instinctual behaviours with 'Hide-and-Seek.' Start indoors and have someone hold your dog while you hide. Progressively make it challenging, hiding behind doors or under the bed.

Transition the game outdoors once your dog is comfortable. Ensure a reward when they find you. For added fun, introduce the element of surprise during outdoor play.

Follow Your Nose: Explore your dog's sense of smell with the 'Follow Your Nose' game. Create a trail using an old cloth soaked in tuna brine, leading to a treat at the end. Vary the location of the treat to keep it interesting. This game mimics your dog's hunting instincts, providing mental stimulation and reinforcing recall in a novel way. I wouldn't advise doing this indoors, it may get a wee bit smelly.

The Two Toy Game: Maintain control and excitement with 'The Two Toy Game.' Present two identical toys, captivating your dog's interest with one and throwing it a short distance. As they grab the first toy, introduce the second and throw it to the opposite side. Think of it a bit like piggy in the middle (another game I used to play as a child). You are the piggy that stays in the middle, creating an interactive recall training session that emphasizes responsiveness.

Target Training: Create a positive association between touch and treats with 'Target Training.' Begin with a closed fist, revealing a treat behind your back. Once your dog investigates and touches your hand, reward them with the hidden treat. Gradually introduce a command word and vary your hand positions for added stimulation.

The Counting Game: Combine training and anticipation with 'The Counting Game.' Count aloud in an enthusiastic tone while placing treats on the ground. Your dog, exploring freely, will come over as you count. Move to a new area and repeat, encouraging quicker responses with each round. If your dog is anything like mine, you will very rarely get past the number 3.

In-Between Game: If multiple family members are present, consider playing the in-between game. Stand several meters apart and call your dog between you, utilising your whistle (see a later chapter regarding whistle training) and body language. This adds an element of fun and competition, strengthening your dog's recall while maintaining engagement.

Funder: Improve focus, engagement, and recall skills with 'Funder.' Stand facing your dog, throw a treat through your legs, and encourage them to go through. Gradually introduce a command word once your dog consistently runs through your legs. This simple yet beneficial game enhances your dog's

Total Recall Training

responsiveness and is also a great place for them to return when you need to get them back on the lead.

Red Light / Green Light: Enhance pacing and recall skills with 'Red Light / Green Light.' Use basic commands like sit, stay, and let's go to cue your dog to stop and start. Reward their stops and gradually introduce different directions and paces, encouraging them to keep up with your movements.

Find It: Encourage your dog's natural sense of smell with 'Find It.' Scatter high-value treats in the grass or leaves, prompting your dog to use their nose to locate them. This game satisfies their basic hunting instincts, providing mental and sensory stimulation.

The Tuggy Tug Tug Game: Make tug-of-war interactive with 'The Tuggy Tug Tug Game.' Use a tug toy or a knotted towel, encouraging your dog to interact. When they let go, reward them and offer the toy back, reinforcing that the game continues even after they release it.

Extreme Fetch: Elevate a classic game with 'Extreme Fetch.' Utilise a frisbee to stimulate your dog's prey drive and enhance their chasing instincts. Begin with short distances, gradually incorporating sit/stay commands for added control. This game transforms a regular game of fetch into an exhilarating experience.

Bubbles: Introduce a playful twist with 'Bubbles.' Blow bubbles in an open area and let your dog chase and pop them. Associate the release of bubbles with a recall command, rewarding your dog when they respond promptly. This game adds a delightful and unpredictable element to recall training.

Flirt Pole: Enhance agility and recall skills with a 'Flirt Pole.' Attach a toy to a long pole and drag it along the ground. Encourage your dog to chase and catch the toy, reinforcing recall by calling them back periodically. This game combines physical activity with responsiveness.

Football: Incorporate 'Football' into your training routine. Roll a small, soft ball and encourage your dog to retrieve it. Use recall commands when calling them back, rewarding their responsiveness. Gradually increase the complexity by introducing dribbling and passing, turning a simple game of fetch into a dynamic training session.

Parkour: Embrace the concept of 'Parkour' during walks. Encourage your dog to interact with the environment creatively. Incorporate natural obstacles like logs or benches, using recall commands to guide them through the course. This game not only strengthens recall but also enhances your dog's problem-solving skills and agility.

These games offer a diverse range of activities to keep your dog engaged, mentally stimulated, and responsive to recall commands. Incorporate them into your routine, adjusting the difficulty as your dog becomes more proficient, and watch as recall training becomes a joyful and rewarding experience for both you and your furry companion. Remember to find the games that your dog LOVES, and don't waste your time on any games that he is not really interested in.

Chapter Eight
Battle Plan

In the previous chapters, we delved into understanding our dogs' strengths, emphasizing the importance of utilising these strengths during walks. Now, let's develop a comprehensive battle plan to enhance recall, ensuring a successful and enjoyable walking experience for both you and your furry companion. This battle plan focuses on the crucial steps before even leaving the house.

Pre-Walk Connection: Your walk doesn't start when you step outside; it begins with a connection at home. Before leaving, take a moment (10 – 15 minutes) to engage with your dog. Connect emotionally, reinforcing your bond, and set a positive tone for the walk ahead. It's essential to establish this connection before even putting on the lead.

Engagement Exercise En Route: On the journey to the park, kickstart engagement exercises with your dog. Encourage them to 'watch' you and reinforce this behaviour with rewards. Initiate pit stops along the way, using these breaks to train, play, and engage with your dog. Conversations, both verbal and non-verbal, contribute to building a strong connection.

Strategic Pit Stops: Pit stops are not just for toilet breaks. Use them strategically to reinforce training, play interactive games, and strengthen the bond with your dog. These stops serve as checkpoints where you connect and redirect your dog's attention positively. It is a constant reminder that you are fun to be around.

Assessing the Park Environment: Arriving at the park, take a moment to assess the environment. Safety should be a priority. If the park is bustling with dogs and distractions that may overwhelm your pup, consider a plan B and head to a quieter location. Setting your dog up for success involves choosing an environment that aligns with their comfort and ability to focus.

Being the Spark: Imagine your energy and enthusiasm as the spark that kindles a fire. Before unleashing your dog, you must be the spark that captures their attention. Consider your excitement as the lighter fluid, building anticipation. This energy is contagious and sets the tone for a lively and engaging walk.

Warm-up with Rewards: Prior to releasing your dog, initiate a warm-up. Let them know you have something they love, whether it's a favourite treat or toy (think about the name game discussed in the previous chapter). This builds anticipation and sets the stage for positive interactions. Offering some slack on the lead, call your dog in a cheerful voice. As they respond, reward them with a treat or their cherished toy. Repeat this process at least five times to ensure their attention is firmly fixed on you.

Variety in Engagement: To maintain their focus, introduce variety in engagement. Throw a ball, scatter treats on the ground, or incorporate other activities that captivate your dog's attention. The goal is to create an environment where your dog is eager to connect with you before being granted the freedom of off lead exploration.

Consistent Reinforcement: Consistency is key in recall training. Reinforce positive behaviour consistently, whether through treats, toys, or verbal praise. The more you reinforce their attention and responsiveness, the stronger the recall training becomes.

Building Confidence: Recall success is not just about attention; it's also about building your dog's confidence. Create an atmosphere where your dog feels secure, understood, and confident in responding to your cues. This confidence reinforces their trust in you and enhances their overall recall abilities.

Crafting a battle plan for recall success involves a holistic approach. It goes beyond the moment of releasing the lead; it encompasses the pre-walk connection, engagement exercises, strategic pit stops, environmental assessment, and being the spark that ignites your dog's attention. This comprehensive strategy ensures a walk that not only exercises your dog physically but also entertains, engages, and fulfils their needs, eliminating conflicts and complications. By implementing this battle plan, you set the stage for a positive and rewarding walking experience, laying the foundation for successful recall training in various environments.

Chapter Nine
Circuit Training

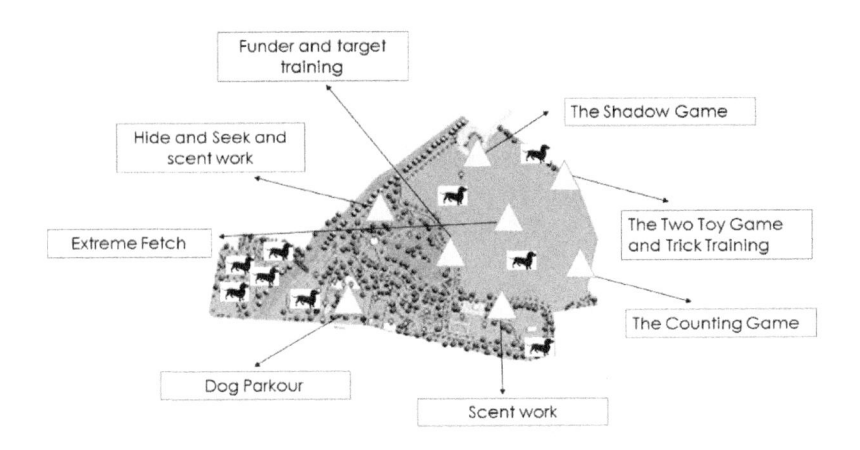

Diagram of a walking route with labelled stations: Funder and target training, The Shadow Game, Hide and Seek and scent work, The Two Toy Game and Trick Training, Extreme Fetch, The Counting Game, Dog Parkour, Scent work.

Much like circuit training for humans, which involves a series of exercises performed in a specific order with brief bursts of activity and rest, circuit training for dogs can be an invaluable addition to your daily walk routine. While we're not advocating for doggy burpees in the park, incorporating circuit training can enhance your dog's focus and deter their attention from wandering towards enticing distractions. This strategic approach, akin to a battle plan, integrates your dog's favourite games, treats, and toys, ensuring an engaging and effective walking experience.

The Importance of Circuit Training: Circuit training, when seamlessly woven into your walk routine, serves as a pivotal element of your battle plan. It not only keeps your dog physically active but also stimulates their mind, preventing boredom and fostering a strong connection with you. By incorporating set locations during your walk where you stop and engage with your dog, you create a structured yet dynamic environment that encourages focus and responsiveness.

Building Your Battle Plan: Crafting an effective battle plan involves identifying specific locations along your walking route where you can conduct short, engaging activities with your dog. These activities can range from games and training sessions to parkour and scent work. By allocating focused time at each station, you maintain a balance between mental and physical stimulation, ensuring a well-rounded experience for your canine companion.

Example of Canine Circuit Training: Below is an example of how you can structure your dog's walk to the park using circuit training. The key is to choose quieter areas to minimize distractions and gradually build engagement, making you the main focal point of their attention. The games we discussed in the previous chapter can also be incorporated into our circuit training, and if you want further games, then be sure to sign up to my online club, The Sandancer Superhero Dog Club.

1. **Station 1 – Warm-up and Engage:** Start your walk with a warm-up session. Use treats, toys, or games to capture your dog's attention. Engage in simple commands, reinforcing their responsiveness.
2. **Station 2 – Parkour Exploration:** Transition to a parkour station where your dog can navigate natural obstacles. Encourage them to climb on logs, jump over low barriers, or balance on designated surfaces. This not only provides physical exercise but also enhances agility and responsiveness.
3. **Station 3 – Training and Commands:**Choose a quiet area for a focused training session. Work on commands such as sit, stay, and recall. Incorporate treats and positive reinforcement to reinforce these commands, making them more reliable in distracting environments.
4. **Station 4 – Scent Work Challenge**: Stimulate your dog's olfactory senses with a scent workstation. Hide treats or toys in the grass or leaves, encouraging your dog to use their nose to locate them. This taps into their natural instincts, providing mental stimulation.
5. **Station 5 – Interactive Playtime:** Dedicate a station to interactive playtime. Use their favourite toys or play games like fetch or tug-of-war. This not only strengthens the bond between you and your dog but also serves as a positive outlet for excess energy.

Adaptability and Flexibility: Remember, this is just a sample circuit training plan. Feel free to customize it based on your dog's preferences, incorporating games, treats, and toys that motivate them. Plans can change, and if you encounter unexpected challenges like a crowded area, calmly redirect to another location and revisit the initial station later.

Circuit training for dogs, integrated into your battle plan, transforms routine walks into dynamic, engaging experiences. By strategically incorporating activities that fulfil your dog's physical and mental needs, you strengthen the bond and responsiveness between you and your furry companion.

Please remember this is not an actual circuit training exercise, and we are not out to burn every last bit of energy out of our dogs, it is more to give you ample opportunity to adapt some games into your walk and to help keep your dog's focus on you, whilst having some fun. Take rests whenever you need to, even if that is putting your dog back on the lead and having a nice stroll to the next zone or to give your dog the chance to check and explore their environment. The main aim of the circuit training is to get your dog in 'park mode', so the battle plan can come to action i.e. dog doesn't bugger off at the first opportunity he gets.

Chapter Ten
Whistle Training

When I welcomed Buddy, a sighthound, into my home, I recognised the challenges that come with recall training for breeds inclined to follow their curiosity. Acknowledging the potential for Buddy to dart off investigating interesting sights, I decided to employ whistle training—a method that had proven highly successful with my previous dog, Lady, until she lost her hearing. Given my profession as a canine behaviourist and the regular group walks organized at Pets2impress, I understood the critical importance of having a reliable recall. This chapter will explore the process of introducing whistle training to your dog, emphasizing its significance in building a strong recall foundation.

The Importance of Whistle Training: A dog that doesn't respond to recall commands can be a source of frustration and concern, especially for a dog trainer. The need for a reliable recall extends beyond personal enjoyment to professional credibility. Whistle training offers a consistent and effective method to ensure your dog responds promptly, fostering a secure and enjoyable walking experience.

Selecting the Right Whistle: Choosing the right whistle is crucial. Having recommended Acme whistles for fifteen years, I've witnessed their reliability. Whether you choose an Acme whistle or another option, prioritize audible whistles over silent ones. A whistle you can hear ensures effective communication and, consequently, successful recall training.

Building a Positive Association: To introduce whistle training, begin indoors with minimal distractions. Arm yourself with high-value treats—something special your dog doesn't regularly have but something that highly motivates them. Much like the excitement a child associates with Santa's sleigh bells, your goal is to link the sound of the whistle with the anticipation of a tasty treat.

Whistle Toot Consistency: Decide on your preferred whistle toot—be it a long blow, short blow, or multiple toots—and maintain consistency. If multiple family members are involved, align on the chosen toot to maintain a cohesive recall experience for your dog. Recognise that while dogs can distinguish between family members, consistency is key in minimizing confusion.

Initial Positive Association Indoors: Practice the whistle indoors, using the chosen toot, followed by an immediate treat. This initial phase establishes a positive association between the whistle sound and the reward. Limit this practice to indoor sessions, ensuring a controlled environment. I would advise spending a couple of minutes, a few times a day, just blowing the whistle and offering a treat so your dog understands exactly what it means when the whistle is blown.

Gradual Introduction of Games: After a few days of successful indoor practice, elevate the excitement by incorporating hide-and-seek games. Move to another room, blow the whistle, and wait for your dog to find you. Praise and reward generously upon successful recall. This not only reinforces the positive association but also engages your dog mentally. You don't need to be locking yourself in cupboards or hiding out in the loft, just moving to another room or calling your dog in from the garden will be enough.

Adding Collar Grab Training: To address the common challenge of grabbing a dog's collar during recall, incorporate collar grab training. When your dog responds to the whistle and finds you during hide-and-seek, grab their collar before issuing the treat. This desensitizes them to collar grabs, making it a routine part of the recall process and ultimately making it easier for you to get your dog back on their lead.

Building a Routine for Outdoor Recall: As your dog becomes accustomed to the whistle and collar grab routine indoors, you pave the way for seamless recall outdoors.

In conclusion, whistle training is a powerful tool for building a strong recall foundation. Acquainting your dog with the whistle's sound and gradually introducing games and collar grab training instil confidence in their responsiveness. This method not only ensures a reliable recall but also strengthens the bond between you and your dog. It is important the whistle acts as a way of getting your attention; they have a choice to make, do they run over to the two dogs chasing each other or do they choose to come back to you? If you are standing with your arms crossed on your phone, I don't fancy your chances. You need to be making yourself fun and engaging, run away, do cartwheels, slap your thighs, and do anything it takes to get them back to you. A whistle is just another tool, but the more you engage with your dog, the less they will stray away from you anyway.

Chapter Eleven
Letting off the Lead

Embarking on the journey of letting your dog off the lead for the first time can be a nerve-wracking experience. Your heart might race, and doubts may cloud your mind, but trust in yourself and your canine companion.

Choosing the Right Environment: Selecting an appropriate environment for the inaugural off lead experience is crucial. Opt for a location with low distractions, avoiding crowded areas like beaches where numerous dogs and people may pose potential challenges. Finding a quiet space ensures that your dog remains focused on you during the initial stages of recall. Equip yourself with high-value treats, toys and, of course, your trusty whistle.

Transitioning with a Long Line: For those apprehensive about unleashing their dog entirely, consider attaching a long line. Long lines provide a sense of freedom while offering control and reassurance for the handler. Available in various lengths, these lines act as a safety net, allowing you to guide or restrain your dog when necessary. They can be easily obtained from local pet shops or online.

The Unveiling: Whether opting for a long line or bravely releasing your dog off the lead, the critical moment has arrived. Allow your dog some freedom, observe as they explore ahead, and then give a resounding blow on your whistle. If your indoor training sessions have been effective, your dog should turn to look at you. Transition seamlessly into one of the fun activities we discussed when we talked about games and circuit training, utilising what excites and motivates your dog.

Keeping the Attention: While the whistle captures your dog's initial attention, maintaining focus is the next challenge. Employ a range of attention-grabbing tactics: jump, slap your thighs, run in the opposite direction, use a high-pitched voice, or entice with their favourite toy or a special item like the magic feather I did with one of the puppies during an outdoor puppy training class. Regardless of the method, the goal is to keep your dog engaged and prevent distractions.

The Chase Game: A common mistake many owners make is only recalling their dog when it's time to go home. This inadvertently conditions the dog to associate recall with the end of playtime, and as you go to grab their collar, they dart off, and before you know it, you are in the middle of a cat and mouse game (or a human and dog game) where the dog is winning. This is another reason why the collar grab is an effective tool. You should be actively calling your dog back to you all of the time, encouraging them to check in with you but if you follow the circuit training advice, they will be actively wanting to check in with you anyway.

The Importance of Recall: Recall is more than just a command; it's a vital lesson that could potentially save your dog's life. Taking the time to train and ensuring it remains enjoyable for your dog is paramount. Thankfully, enclosed dog parks or fields are now available for hire, providing a controlled environment for recall practice and boosting handler confidence.

Maintaining Engagement: Avoid becoming a disengaged owner constantly glued to your phone during walks. Actively engage with your dog, utilising body language, enthusiastic calls, and positive reinforcement. Keep the experience fun, maintaining your dog's focus and interest.

Final Tips: Remember, the whistle captures attention, body language sustains it, the middle command guides, and high-value treats reward. Gradually introduce distractions, building up your dog's recall capabilities over time. With consistent effort and positive reinforcement, you'll foster a reliable recall that allows your dog to enjoy off-leash adventures safely.

Chapter Twelve
The Unleashing Freedom

In the intricate tapestry of canine training, one thread stands out as both a cornerstone and a lifeline—recall. The ability to call your dog back reliably is not just a command but a fundamental skill that fosters a profound connection, solidifies the human-canine relationship and paves the way for a harmonious coexistence. In this comprehensive conclusion, we delve into the multifaceted aspects of recall, exploring the significance of connection, relationship-building, engagement strategies, whistle training, circuit training, and the role of interactive games in achieving a robust and reliable recall.

The Heartbeat of Connection:

At the heart of every successful recall is a connection forged in the crucible of mutual understanding and respect. The foundation of this connection lies in the relationship between the owner and their canine companion. Unlike traditional training approaches that rely solely on obedience, a connection-based recall transcends commands, reaching into the realm of companionship, trust, and shared experiences. This connection becomes the compass guiding the dog back to its owner, even in the face of enticing distractions.

Building the Relationship:

A recall that hinges on a robust relationship is not built overnight; it's a gradual process nurtured through shared activities, quality time spent together, and a keen understanding of each other's needs. The relationship evolves from the cultivation of mutual respect, empathy, and a genuine friendship. Recognising the unique personality of each dog and adapting training methods accordingly lays the groundwork for a relationship built on trust, a key element in ensuring a reliable recall.

Engagement: The Two-Way Street:

Engagement in the context of recall is a dynamic two-way street where both parties actively participate. The owner's role extends beyond being the commander; they become the conductor orchestrating a symphony of interaction, communication, and shared joy. Dogs naturally gravitate towards activities that align with their instincts and desires, and a skillful owner leverages this knowledge to keep the dog willingly engaged. The chapter on engagement explores how to make walks more than just walks, transforming them into adventures rich with sensory experiences, training opportunities, and mental stimulation.

Whistle Training: A Harmonious Melody of Communication:

Introducing a whistle into the training repertoire adds a layer of clarity and consistency to recall efforts. Whistle training, as discussed in a previous chapter, is more than a tool for catching attention; it becomes a harmonious melody in the communication between owner and dog. The choice of the right whistle and the strategic pairing of its sound with high-value treats lay the groundwork for a positive association. The step-by-step process, from indoor conditioning to outdoor applications, serves as a testament to the power of positive reinforcement in creating a responsive recall.

Circuit Training: A Journey Within the Journey:

Circuit training, both for humans and dogs, involves a sequence of exercises strategically designed for short bursts of activity interspersed with brief rests. Translating this concept into the realm of dog recall transforms the walk into a journey within the journey. Circuit training for dogs, as outlined in a previous chapter, incorporates various elements like games, parkour, training, and scent work. The aim is not just exercise but a holistic approach that fulfils the dog's physical and mental needs while eliminating conflicts and complications.

The Power of Interactive Games:

Interactive games form a crucial part of recall training. These games are not just for entertainment but serve as valuable tools for reinforcing recall skills. In this section, we explored a myriad of games, each designed to enhance specific aspects of recall, from the "Name Game" that redefines the dog's association with its name to engaging activities like hide-and-seek, fetch variations, and tug-of-war. These games, when woven into the fabric of recall training, make learning enjoyable, cementing the bond between owner and dog.

Conclusion: A Symphony of Connection and Freedom:

As we reach the crescendo of this exploration into dog recall, it's evident that a reliable recall is not a solitary note but a symphony. It is a melody composed of the threads of connection, relationship, engagement, whistle training, circuit training, and interactive games. The importance of a strong connection cannot be overstated; it is the lifeline that ensures the dog willingly returns, not out of obedience but out of a shared understanding and love.

Recall is not a singular command shouted across a field; it is a multifaceted skill that requires a holistic approach. Building a relationship steeped in mutual respect and empathy forms the foundation. Engaging the dog in meaningful activities, leveraging the power of a well-trained whistle, incorporating circuit training into walks, and infusing joy through interactive games contribute to the richness of the recall experience.

In the grand finale of this journey, recall emerges not just as a command but as a liberating force, granting dogs the freedom to explore while providing owners with the peace of mind that their loyal companions will return, not out of obligation but because the bond between them is unbreakable. The journey to a reliable recall is a symphony, and each element harmonizes to create a melody of connection, understanding, and freedom that resonates through the lead, transcending mere obedience to forge a partnership that lasts a lifetime.

In the heart of a fulfilling and joyous life for our dogs lies the essence of enrichment. Enrichment is at the forefront of my daycare, where the well-being and happiness of attending dogs are paramount.

Enrichment is not merely an afterthought but a cornerstone of their experience, creating an environment that nurtures their physical, mental, and emotional needs. From interactive toys to sensory experiences, the daycare is a playground of stimuli, ensuring that each dog is not just occupied but genuinely fulfilled.

The concept of enrichment extends beyond the confines of a dedicated space; it should seamlessly integrate into the daily routines of every dog owner. You should be adding enrichment strategies during walks with your dog. The walk then becomes more than just a physical exercise; it transforms into an opportunity for mental stimulation, exploration, and bonding, and as a result, you will have a much happier dog.

The benefits are multifold – a tired, content, and mentally stimulated dog and a stronger, more enriching connection between you and your dog.

Enrichment is not a luxury; it is a necessity for the holistic well-being of our dogs. The profound impact that enrichment has on your dog's physical health, mental agility, and overall happiness will become evident. Whether in a specialized daycare or on the daily walks you share, enrichment emerges as the key to unlocking the full potential of your dog's joyful and vibrant life. Embrace the power of enrichment, and watch as your dog transforms into the happy, stimulated, and fulfilled companion you've always envisioned, plus one that comes back to you too, winner, winner, chicken dinner!

Post Walk

Throughout this book, we have looked at how to have a reliable recall, how to make walks into adventures, how to implement games into your dog's training and how to make coming back to you the first choice for your dog. If you have followed your battle plan and implemented the advice I have shared with you in this book, then you should have a dog with much less energy. Let's not waste this time as now is a great time to practice with your dog's on lead training on your way home from the park (See my other book, Take the Lead for the Perfect Recall) as well as focusing on tricks that require your dog to stay still. Don't forget dogs are always learning, and once the lead is back on, don't lose your dog's focus. Keep working with your dog, there is plenty of time for rest when you get back home and snuggle up on the settee together watching Netflix. If you fancy a good series, I would highly recommend Cobra Kai, a personal favourite of mine.

Just remember the ingredients required for a Victoria Sponge are vital to make that perfect cake, and the steps we have discussed within this book are also just as important, so make sure you do not miss any sections out. Recall doesn't happen overnight; it takes time and patience, but the more time you invest in your dog's recall, the stronger and more reliable it will become. Just remember to follow the steps in this book, but most importantly, have fun with your dog.

As I have mentioned Victoria Sponge cake more than once during this book, just in case you fancy making your own Victoria Sponge, the crucial ingredients needed are

- 200g caster sugar
- 200g softened butter
- 4 eggs, beaten
- 200g self-raising flour
- 1 tsp baking powder
- 2 tbsp milk

For the Filling

- 100g butter, softened
- 140g icing sugar, sifted
- drop vanilla extract (optional)
- half a 340g jar of good-quality strawberry jam
- icing sugar, to decorate

Chapter Thirteen
The Sandancer Superhero Dog Club

I have mentioned The Sandancer Superhero Dog Club a number of times throughout this book and thought it was only right I actually explain further what being a member of the club can do for you. The Sandancer Superhero Dog Club is where dog training transcends the pages of this book into a dynamic online community dedicated to nurturing the superhero within your furry companion. As a token of appreciation for purchasing this book, reading it, and hopefully enjoying it (don't forget that 5* Amazon review), you'll find an exclusive bonus section at the end of this book, offering two months of complimentary access to my online club. Becoming a member unlocks a plethora of benefits, ensuring not only the transformation of your dog but also fostering a lifelong bond between you and your four-legged friend.

One of the key advantages of our online club is the ongoing support you'll receive. In the dog training world, consistency is key, and our club provides a continuous support system to guide you through every step of your training journey. As the founder of the club, I'm dedicated to being there for my members, offering insights, answering queries, and providing personalized advice to address the unique needs of your canine companion.

The club is designed to offer a rich and diverse learning experience. Monthly Q&A sessions provide a direct line to me, allowing you to seek guidance on specific challenges you may encounter. To further enhance your knowledge, I host monthly teleclasses featuring esteemed guest speakers, delving into a range of dog-related topics, from behaviour and training to health and nutrition.

For a sense of community and shared experiences, our online forum is a hub where members can connect, share stories, and seek advice from fellow dog enthusiasts. The camaraderie doesn't end there; we regularly conduct monthly challenges that add an element of fun to the learning process. These challenges not only deepen your connection with your dog but also contribute to a positive training environment.

Our private Facebook support group is a safe space where members can engage in discussions, seek advice, and celebrate victories, creating a supportive network of like-minded individuals. The vault of resources is a treasure trove, housing a variety of videos and online courses that cover a spectrum of training topics. From the foundational "Ready Steady Recall" and "Lead Training" to the whimsical "Dancing with Dogs" and specific challenges like "Help My Dog is a Devil with Other Dogs" and "Bark No More," there's a wealth of knowledge at your fingertips.

To cater to our newest furry friends, we've curated the "Puppy Pawfection Course," a comprehensive guide to laying the foundation for a well-behaved and happy canine companion. In essence, The Sandancer Superhero Dog Club is more than an online platform; it's a community where you and your dog can thrive, learn, and grow together. After delving into the pages of this book, signing up to our online club is the next step toward unlocking your dog's superhero potential and ensuring a fulfilling and harmonious relationship between you and your canine sidekick. Don't take my word for it, have a read of what some of the members think about being a part of the club.

"I have worked with Tim for quite a few years now, beginning in log down when he helped me change my relationship with my dog for the better.

When I heard about his new online dog group, the 'Sandancer super hero dog club', I just knew we had to be part of it. Alfie, a beagle, was nine years old when the group began; I had seen such positive changes with Alfie. I felt being part of the group was giving Alfie the best life that I could give him.

We now have another pup joining our family. I have read and highlighted important parts of Tim's book 'The South Shields Puppy Play Book'. I feel we made a lot of mistakes with Alfie, and with Tim's help, we have rectified our errors and now have an amazing relationship with him.

Alfie still occasionally gets upset when he sees other dogs, but he is so much better than he was, and he still barks at people coming to and into our home. However, just recently, he is getting better at barking to let us know and then running to his spot and letting us answer the door. This is ongoing work. But we will get there!

We are so looking forward to Quincey joining us, and we know Tim will be an amazing support with whatever difficulties we have when Quincey joins our family. Quincey is already booked on to Tim's puppy class.

Thank you again, Tim, you are absolutely fabulous!" **Jill Jones, Human of Alife and soon Quincey**

"I joined the Sand Dancer Club when it started a couple of months ago, and I am so pleased that I did. I have known Tim for a while now through puppy class, some 1-1 training, and my dog loves daycare; the work that Tim has done with Murphy and the advice given has been fantastic. The most telling point for me, as well as seeing the improvements in Murphy's behaviour, is the fact that my dog, who doesn't easily trust people or want them to touch him, loves Tim and will always run over with excitement to greet him!

The Sand Dancer Club has lots of advice as well as lots of fun activities to do with your dog that build on focus and having a great relationship with your dog. For me, one of the best things is that the group is so supportive of each other, offering praise and suggestions when people ask for advice, and Tim is always quick to respond to any questions asked. I really enjoy the question-and-answer live sessions as, quite often, the questions others have also result in activities that will help in lots of different situations.

I have enjoyed some really good online training through the Club, which was both fun and informative. Murphy and I love the monthly challenges and learning new things. We are really enjoying the benefits of being in the Sand Dancer Club," **Nicola Mackins, Human of Murphy**

"We first started with Pets2impress at puppy school, where Winston attended and LOVED it. We recently joined The Sandancer Superhero Dog Club with our free trial (about 3months after finishing puppy school), and not only have we kept it up, but we wish we'd done it sooner. The love Tim shows for the pups in his care shines through everything he does, so it's not surprising that his service is in such high demand.

We recently had a phone call with Tim to discuss Winston's separation anxiety, and not only did it put my mind at ease, it's given me the tools to help Winston feel at ease being alone. Tim talked me through everything and reassured me that it wouldn't be an overnight process, which really helped as it's so easy to feel like you're failing when the steps are so small. We're still working on it; he's loving his pen now and happily plays in there when I clean or have to do some work at night, but I know if we hit a roadblock, Tim is always on the other end of the phone.

I couldn't recommend Tim and Pets2impress enough. It's a huge deal to put your pup into someone's hands to look after when you have to work, and while we don't currently use daycare as I'm lucky enough to be able to take Winston to work with me if I need to, I wouldn't hesitate to trust Tim and his team with my fur baby!" **Claire Rarity, Human of Winston**

"Bronte already enjoys going to Tim's daycare after having completed puppy school with him too, so when he created the Sanddancer Superhero Dog Club, I joined as I was keen to continue and develop Bronte's training to run alongside daycare and some 1-2-1 training that we have also had with Tim. Bronte is a very friendly, happy and generally easy-going dog, but as a young border terrier, she also shows some of the instinctual behaviours of the breeds that have made certain things like recall training difficult at times, and she can also be quite stubborn and mischievous if she gets bored! By joining the Sanddancer Superhero Dog Club, I have access to so many online training courses that have helped me with these things and the monthly challenges etc, give me new fun ways of tiring Bronte out in the house both mentally and physically, so that she is nicely settled.
The Club is way more than just for training however - it is a wonderful community of like-minded dog owners who all want to learn about and bring out the very best in their dogs and who all really support each other. Led by Tim, who is not just very experienced and knowledgeable but also highly entertaining, we are all able to share our experiences and our progress and really learn from each other in a really supportive environment.
I highly recommend the Club to anyone thinking of joining - you will not regret it!" **Kate Henderson, Human of Bronte**

I decided to introduce this new online training club because I had so much fun with the online courses I ran during the COVID-19 lockdowns. I also got to a point where I had a huge waiting list for my 1-1 clients, and I thought with an online club, I could help more people and their dogs all at once. Plus on a practical note, there is only so much Tim Jackson to go around. I hope to continue growing the club and club members over time. I would love for you to become my next member; check out the bonus section for your first two months free.

Bonus Section

I hope you have enjoyed reading this book, and I hope it has left you feeling motivated and ready to kickstart your dog's recall training. The best results come to those who take action and are patient with their dog during the training stages.

I do appreciate that there is only so much you can take away from a book, which is why I have decided to share some free gifts with you.

- **My first gift to you is two months FREE access to The Sandancer Superhero Dog Club.**

Visit the Pets2impress website, **www.pets2impress.com** and sign up under the dog club section. Upon checkout, enter the code 9GAJMBTV to claim your two months free, and if you find it's not for you, then cancel at any time.

- **My second gift to you is a free copy of the Pets2impress Training Guide. This will really help give you a head start with your dog's foundation training, even if it is just a refresher.**

Visit the link below to grab your copy
https://mailchi.mp/17e466208370/free-training-guide

- **My third gift to you is a series of video tutorials to use alongside your training guide.**

Visit the link below to download the video tutorials
https://mailchi.mp/66a2c0b8756f/puppy-bonus-tutorials

- **My fourth gift to you is a free download of the South Shields Dog-Friendly Map**

Visit the link below to grab your copy
https://mailchi.mp/aa6c688ef631/your-dog-friendly-guide-to-south-shields

- **My Fifth gift to you is a free PDF version of Recycle the Recycling, which will give you some ideas for some homemade brain games to use with your puppy**

Visit the link below to grab your copy
https://mailchi.mp/c877fefbe914/recycletherecycling

- **My sixth gift to you is a PDF version of one of my other books, Take the Lead for the Perfect Recall**

Click on the link to download your copy
https://mailchi.mp/9c9bd5dff7e7/l4aenw58ch

- **And my seventh gift to you is a free webinar entitled, An Introduction to Scent Work**

Click on the link to watch the webinar
https://mailchi.mp/cc93605a09d7/an-introduction-to-scent-work

As a thank you for these invaluable gifts, please feel free to leave a glowing review on Amazon for me. If you make use of your two months FREE access to The Sandancer Superhero Dog Club, you will gain immediate access to my online courses, so be sure to sign up and get watching.

About The Author

Tim Jackson started his career working with animals as a veterinary auxiliary nurse. He trained and qualified as a veterinary nurse in 2007 at Myerscough College. He was promoted to Head veterinary nurse and spent a number of years helping animals and their owners.

In 2008, Tim launched Pets2impress, a company that took the region by storm. What began as a pet-sitting service soon expanded to offer a variety of services.

In 2014, Tim took the decision to leave his position as Head Veterinary nurse to expand Pets2impress, a difficult decision but a necessary one to help expand and grow Pets2impress.

Tim has completed multiple animal behaviour courses, including the Think Dog Certificates and has a Diploma in Animal Behaviour. He passed each of these with a distinction, and the knowledge he gained from these, combined with his extensive nursing experience, allowed him to offer one-on-one training sessions for all problem behaviours, utilising only positive, reward-based training programmes.

This is a fun and stress-free method of training, which is easy to learn and rapidly achieves fantastic results. In its most basic form, it is a method of communication that is very clear for the dog. Examples of problem behaviours which Tim is able to assist with include separation anxiety, basic and foundation training, including lead and recall training, dog-on-dog aggression and other anxiety-related issues; however, no problem is too small or too big for Tim.

In 2015, Tim opened a state-of-the-art daycare facility, offering a safe, enriching and stimulating environment for dogs whilst their owners are out at work. His experience as a qualified veterinary nurse, dog trainer and canine behaviourist gave him a comprehensive understanding that all dogs have different physical and emotional needs, allowing daycare sessions to be tailor-made to suit each individual.

Tim runs his daycare as close to a nursery setting as possible and, therefore, follows a daily schedule as closely as possible. This is extremely beneficial to the dogs in his care as it has been well documented that dogs thrive off predictability, and it has positive effects on both their behaviour and mental well-being.

A typical day at the daycare centre includes free play, walks outside for a change of scenery, training time, top-to-tail examinations and quiet time, as rest is extremely important to prevent overstimulation, which can have a negative impact on both behaviour and physical condition. In October 2019, Tim launched an additional package to the daycare service, the doggy 'adventure' daycare, to offer dogs further opportunities to receive physical and mental stimulation whilst in daycare, as well as receive the other benefits daycare has to offer. In June 2020, Tim launched two additional packages to the daycare service, The Scent Space and School Trips; as with the adventure daycares, these were designed to allow dogs further opportunities to receive physical and mental stimulation. In September 2020, Tim launched his brand new unique daycare membership club, which is filled with so many benefits for owners and their dogs. Tim also launched picnics, and in 2023, Tim launched magical Mondays at daycare and Forest School Fridays, as well as a brand new 1-1 level on the daycare membership packages.

Tim is well known for his sense of humour and love and dedication to the welfare of all animals. Tim has owned several animals over the years, including a rescue tarantula (which he was absolutely terrified of), an iguana, bearded dragons, cats, hamsters, rats, mice, fish and dogs.

Tim's mission in life is to help owners who struggle with their dogs prevent them from ending up in shelters.

When not working, Tim can be seen swapping Doggy Daycare for Daddy Daycare. Tim loves nothing more than spending time with his four adorable children. He can also be found out walking his dogs Buddy and Bea and every now and then enjoys a nice pint at the local pub.

To find out more about Tim and Pets2impress please visit the Pets2impress website **www.pets2impress.com**

Other Books by the Author

Available to purchase from **www.pets2impress.com** and Amazon

Dog Training Book

Help! My dog is a Devil with Other Dogs

Help! My dog doesn't like being left alone

Take the Lead for the Perfect Recall

The South Shields Puppy Playbook

Acknowledgments

As this is my fifth book, there are so many people I would like to thank, so many people who have supported me over the years and pushed me to always try harder. I definitely forgot to say thanks to certain people in my last four books, oops... I'll try harder in this book.

My first thanks must go to my adorable dogs that I have had over the years, it is thanks to them that I found my love for dog training and dog behaviour. Gone but never forgotten I would like to dedicate this book to my first dog Pip, Lady, Rosie and my two current dogs, Buddy and Bea.

To my Mam and Dad, who are always there when I need them. I wouldn't be the person I am today without them.

Special thanks to Rebecca and my four adorable children, Sienna, Harvey, Darcey and Alfie. They give me a purpose to continue working hard.

Special thanks to my karate Crew, Sam, Jo, Emma and Chris. These guys are some of the best friends I have ever had.

Special thanks to Shihan Mark Purcell and Sensei Blane Stamps, who have been so supportive during my karate journey and encouraged me to keep training hard.

Special thanks to my good friend Annouska Muzyczuk, who has always stuck by me through thick and thin. She is one of my longest friends and the one person I turn to when I need help.

A special shout out to Shannon Nixon, who I worked with during my time in practice, who worked for Pets2impress for a number of years and who now has her very own successful dog-walking business.

A special shout out to Chloe Boundy, whom I met when she completed her placement work at Pets2impress; I always enjoyed our pizza special Thursdays. Chloe too has her very own successful dog-walking business.

To my mentor, Dominic Hodgson, the Pet Biz Wiz from Grow Your Pet Business Fast, for his guidance and support and for continuing to push me forward.

To the staff at Pets2impress, Lyndsey, Naomi, Alicia and Karen 1. For putting up with me and for laughing at my not-so-funny jokes and 2. For your support, enthusiasm and shared love you have for the dogs in our care. I couldn't do the job I do without my amazing team. 3. For going along with every crazy idea I have

A special thanks to Joanna Hicklin for her amazing help with the Pets2impress Puppy School.

To my Pets2impress clients, who have been loyal to Pets2impress all these years. I would not be where I am today without your support, recommendations and dedication.

To the veterinary staff, who I used to work with for their support and recommendations over the years. They certainly had to put up with a lot from me, from singing constantly to winding each of them up on a daily basis. I certainly miss working with them every day.

My final thanks must go to you. Thank you for choosing this book and spending the time to read it. I hope you found it useful, and I hope you start to action the points made in this book. My mission is to try and prevent as many dogs from ending up in shelters as possible and to help dogs live happy, enriching lives and if this book helps others, then I can sleep well at night. I ask if you found this book useful that, you leave a review on Amazon… I will accept no less than a 5-star rating.